Ultimate Wisdom Code I

IDEAS

I0115320

Copyright

Copyright © 2014 Emilton K.

Contact author at:

wisdomcode12@gmail.com

ULTIMATE

WISDOM CODE

Fountain of Ultimate Peace, Happiness

and Greatness

By

Emilton K.

ACKNOWLEDGEMENTS

My utmost thanks to God for inspiration.
My sincere thanks to Pr. Xavier Dijon, my intellectual mentor, who with the diligence of a miner, extracted from my darkness that which was bright and noble.

My sincere gratitude to Pr. Ernest-Marie Mbonda, Pr. Marie-Therese Mengue, Dr. Steven Nur Ahmed and Pr. Claude Kiamba who with patience and trust, instilled in me the value of hard work and knowledge.

Without the support of my professional mentors, this initiative wouldn't have been a success: Emmanuel Kiven, Nyeck Cirille, Dzemo Romuald Ngong.

I would like to express gratitude to Ellison Yufenyuy, DJ Krasev, Andrew Berinyuy for patiently reading through this work.

My appreciations to all those who have contributed to my understanding of the world and of life as a whole: Pr. B.I.C. Ijomah, Bruce A. Taylor, Patricia Vroom, Stephen Chapman, Yefenyuy Ellison and Yufenyuy Stella, Karen Jilavdaryan, Eric McCalla, Shane Oregon Patrick, Jessica Zweng, Daljinder Singh, Sanchez Victor, Sean-Paul Simpson, Mbilam Samson, Javier Gracia, Lambert Kogo, Joseph Ter Tir, Festus Nkenbeza, Frankline P, MarinesJuarz, Baoteng Polson Rudolph, Delphine Ambe, Joseph, Alain N., Pr. Claude Lah, Madina, Ngeuleu Isidore, Mark Ndifor, Hernandez, Milini Chin-Che, Jude Wirnkar, Guy Thomas, Zapora K. Mason, Hans de Marie, Robbs, Cook, Broussard, Mei A. Chen, Asheri N., Samuel I. Crooks Richard, D.J. Krasev, Martha Bongfen, Allan Ndwega, Lukong Elvis, Isaac Kewong, Paul Tentow, Arsene Ngozogo, Yvonne Mboume, Kinyuy Belinda, Ade

Sebastian, Chitor, Chitor Stanley Chinyeaka, Delly Dee. Keneth Ambe, Nge Valentine, Marianne Nsalav, Albert Ndze, Macky le Baobab, Frederich Ngan, Jenny Nsoyori, Andrew Berinyuy, Nina Forgwe, Patrick Kalala, Daniel Tshimbalanga, Mokia Fomonyuy, Dzemo Romuald, Toussaint Epekou, Henrick Moafo, Max Sainclair Mbida, Eileen Basang, Richard Taun, Ngwa John, Terry Hudson Sola, White Sharnice, Anthony Koffa, Athanasius CYP, Darlington, Jude Jehla Wirnkar, Guy Thomas, Abeng Emmanuel Hala Madrid, Athanasius Uwakwe, Obidiegwu Sandra.

Gadsden, Alabama, U.S.A., Nov. 28. 2012

PREFACE

When I first met Emilton K. in Arizona back in 2012, he struck me as a quiet and introspective man. Little did I know that behind that calm exterior lay hidden a maelstrom of furious, incessant mental activity that never seemed to take off a day. What's more? He turned out to be the kind of person who is actually able to verbalize and put down into words the catchy, engaging, and stimulating aphorisms you are about to read with a clarity and humor few possess.

When I started reading what Emilton K. was writing, I couldn't help but compare his style and take on existential matters with that of Nietzsche. Not a bad comparison, indeed. His axioms and dictums make the reader pause and reflect, then reread and think again about the deeper meaning hidden in the carefully worded, almost playful truisms and adages the author has crafted.

Indeed, Emilton K. has that extra gear when it comes to language, to say nothing of his uncanny grasp of daily life's ironies and lessons learned the hard way.

But perhaps most amazing, in the context of the undeniably American background of Emilton's writing, is the fact that his wisdom is international, if not universal.

Time honored and life tested wisdom cannot be pigeonholed into being of one nationality, ethnicity, religion, or culture. It should be, as is the case with the Wisdom Code I, timeless. I find that in this gem of a book, it really is.

So you'll definitely, enjoy these tasty bits of wisdom regardless of your origin, and perhaps you will discover yourself in the process!

DJ Krastev, **Writer and Editor**

"I was excited that ..., he had assembled what looks like the wisdom of the ages. Perhaps in the tradition of John P. Bradley who edited the International Dictionary of Thoughts, Emilton has begun on a modest note. This edition is the first of such works in this part of the world. The thoughts are brilliantly arranged and send the reader into a mood that opens a vista of life." –

By Prof. B.I.C. Ijomah, PhD (Northwestern)

DEDICATION

In loving memory of my father **WIRNGO EVARESTUS TAR** *from whom I learned that art of ultimate wisdom through his life of hard work, dedication, love, sacrifice, patience, humility, forgiveness and silence.*

May you find peace in the resurrection of the Lord and also remain alive though this work of art in which you have breathed life as a testimony of your wisdom.

ADVICE

A good adviser is good; too many good advisers, bad.

Who is the adviser of your adviser? The former is the real adviser.

Unskillful and lazy advisers are more dangerous than the enemy and more problematic than the problems they're called to solve.

Those who like giving advice often hate receiving it.

Gossip often starts in the form of an advice. That is why those who seek advice from everyone gossip, considering their sad activity as a form of piety.

ANGER

Envy leads to one error. Jealousy leads to two errors. Anger leads to three errors. It is the nature of evil to attract more evil.

It is when we are angry that we shamelessly gust the ugliest thoughts that we have always had on others, which does not only make others ugly but also makes us uglier.

The first thing to do when you are angry is to keep silence. The second thing is to keep silence, and the third thing is to keep silence.

It is permitted to be angry but not permitted to act with anger.

Worry is better than anger; however, both can kill.

Getting angry for the right reason, at the right time, and in the right way is indeed virtue.

Each triumph over anger is a step towards success and peace.

Anger is the revenge we give to ourselves when we fail to let love triumph.

BEAUTY

When beauty loses its sublime meaning, it is called sexy.

When the beauty of a woman is seen on her face, a man's
beauty is in his brains.
If the woman's beauty is in her butts, that of the man is in
his pockets.
And when a woman is judged beautiful by virtue of her
breasts, a man's beauty is measured in his smartness.

Beauty is like a brand that creates distinction in form
but does not necessarily change the quality or nature
of the product.

Beauty is meaning. A less pretty woman with more
meaning is more beautiful, while a prettier one with less
meaning is less beautiful. Meaning is determined by
behavior.

Nowadays, beauty is a commodity that is sold to the
highest bidder.

Beauty is geometrically distributed, but the way it is
capitalized is the same.

BEHAVIOR

The only thing that is consistent in human behavior is inconsistency.

It is impossible to always please others without hurting oneself.

People are judged for *who* they are and for *what* they are. The first is by virtue of what they are for themselves, while the second is by virtue of what they are for others. Because people are always influenced by the way they affect others, and not strictly by whom they are for themselves, they are consequently judged for *what* they are and not for *who* they are.

Poor habits are cultivated in joy, but they are destroyed in tears.

Bad behavior is not only addictive but contaminative. Good behavior is not only compulsive but also contagious.

BEGGING

Begging is the sanction we inflict on our being when we refuse the lesser sanctions of hard work, sacrifice, suffering and pain.

He who refuses to beg in the most difficult situation will definitely find a solution to his problem. He who refuses a cheap solution in a difficult situation will certainly find a sustainable solution to his challenges.

What do beggars think when others beg from them? "Are you tempting me?"

Borrowing corrupts. Begging is corruption in itself.

Beggars are never respected, no matter how cheerful their givers may appear. If they should know what their cheerful givers think about them, they would choose otherwise.

Begging is dangerous. Not because those who beg are in danger from what they lack, but more so because they are in danger from those who offer what they lack.

Begging is bad, but is be permitted and encouraged in three situations: to beg for wisdom, forgiveness, or grace.

BLESSING

Rest is a blessing. Work is a great blessing. Hard work is a greater blessing. If rest is a blessing, then idleness is a curse.

He who is not blessed is he who is not alive. He who does not bless is he who refuses to be alive. And he who refuses blessings is he who kills himself.

BORROW AND DEBTS

Three bad things that can happen to a man:

1) To live in debt, 2) to refuse to pay debts, 3) to be unable to pay debts.

   The first is sad. The second is shameful. The third is pitiful.

Never live above your means, but never wait for [all] the means to dare on what you want in life. Life offers its own means for those who dare sincerely.

The only debt that is honorable is the debt of love.

CHARITY

Knowledge that is shared increases. When it is kept to oneself, it reduces.

The dance of love is charity, and the music of wisdom is truth.

Any gift offered out of pity is followed by an insult; but any gift made out of *love* is followed by respect.

The attitude of giving purifies, while that of receiving corrupts.

It is not virtue to accept charity all the time.

Charity is vice when it is done for the exclusive good of the giver.

Charity is not eleemosynary. The first is an outflow from inside towards unconditional kindness, while the second is an outward flow of kindness which is generally conditional.

COMPARISONS

Pleasure is arithmetic. Happiness is geometric. Peace is Euclidean.

The noblest duties in societies are assigned to politics and religion. That is why they are similar: the first capitalizes on the human strength to defend man in society, while the second capitalizes on human weakness to defend man from himself and from society. Historically, they both triumph with the help of each other.

Happiness and pleasure? The first is perpetually constant while the second is constantly fading. The first is light while the second is delight. Light and delight are similar because they console and encourage us to continue this obscure, complex, tough, and rough journey through life.

Eternity and temporality are characterized by one essential thing – presence. Eternity is perpetual presence while temporality is a mutable presence between past and future.

Existence is presence.

Truth and falsity are not what they are in themselves, but often what we make them to be.

Faith and Faithful? The first is constancy in belief while the second is constancy in action. Paradoxically, we have those who have faith but are not faithful while others are faithful but they don't have faith.

Compassion is a sentiment of love. Pity is a sentiment of contempt.

A tithe is a tax while a tax is a tithe. All are the same; they differ mainly in the name and the way they are being used.

There is a close similarity between unfaithfulness, promiscuity, and prostitution. All are about interest and differ only in the price.

There is a close connection between a prostitute and a virgin: the first struggles to survive while the second survives in a struggle. In fact, they both struggle and they both survive.

COUNTRY-NATION

A tax is a due that a stakeholder regularly invests in his company for its sustainable welfare, as a sign of acknowledgement of an individual possible welfare and as a manifestation of willingness for a collective welfare.

Stereotypes:

An American is someone who respects the constitution.

A British is someone who respects the crown.

A French is someone who respects his culture.

A Chinese is someone who respects an ideology.

A Russian is someone who respects the government.

A Japanese is someone who respects the emperor.

An African is someone who respects his tradition.

What is the role of the State? Simple: federating everybody's resources for the welfare of the individual, and capitalization of individual resources for the welfare of everyone.

The State is the highest rationalization of social organization characterized by the rule of law.

A citizen who has no love for his nation is more dangerous than an alien. In reality, he is an alien with a borrowed nationality.

The greatest enemies of the State are those who think that their ideas are so indispensable for the State's welfare that others should be put to silence.

Nations are not what they ought to be. They are designs of people who fashion them to be what they want them to be.

Our forefathers fought with their sweat, tears, and blood for the peace, freedom, and prosperity of this land. Today, we fight for peace, freedom, and prosperity by hanging in bars, nightclubs, or by sitting idle on couches, watching television – beer on one hand and cigarette on the other – hoping for things to get better. We have dangerously betrayed our fathers... and we have ourselves to blame when things turn dark.

Nothing is as shameful as ruling over poor citizens.

A poor nation is vulnerable to danger. A corrupt nation is danger in itself.

The progress of nations depends on *design* and *opportunity*. The first is determined by what we create, while the second is exploiting the possibilities of what others create. Since the first depends on us, there is always a reason to hope, and since the second depends on others, there is often incertitude.

22

Theoretically, the European Union is an organization. Practically, it is an empire resurrected from the defunct central and axis empires in order to facilitate and expand the imperial rule.

The most precious of all resources in a nation is not gold or diamonds, but the citizens themselves, who through hard work, discipline, sacrifice and solidarity can turn their *resource-less* land into a paradise. These citizens can equally be a dangerous factor who dilapidate all vital resources of the land, including each other, leaving the nation to be a holocaust zone where everybody's dream is laid to waste through laziness, greed, corruption and selfishness.

Nations are born through blood, pain, and sacrifice but die through pleasure, laziness, and greed.

A nation grows from what it produces, and dies from what it consumes.

Progress is expensive, maintaining progress is very expensive, and refusing progress is still most expensive.

The Decalogue of the State

i.   Thou shalt love me and have none other but me.

ii.   Thou shalt not make false images of me anywhere or pay tribute to any other for I am a jealous State. iii. Thou shalt not take my sovereignty and fame in vain.

iv.   Remember national days, property, and keep them honored.

v.   Honor thy government and laws so that thy security may be ensured

vi.   Thou shalt not refuse to pay taxes because failure to do so is murder to the State.

vii.   Thou shalt not engage in forgery, illegal business or trafficking.

viii.   Thou shalt not bear false witness against thy citizen

ix.   Thou shalt not covet thy citizens property or pay-check

x.   Thou shalt not covet thy citizen's lover.

Thus says the State all sovereign.

A nation can be destroyed either from inside – weakening its laws, or from outside by strengthening its dependence.

Running any State is always very expensive because its needs are luxurious and everyone wants a maximum share of its wealth. This often leads to bankruptcy or high-debts. Unless we all pledge to contribute more, ask less, and spend moderately, this situation will not change.

A nation that depends on another for a fair proportion of its food is a nation on postponed starvation. A nation that depends on another for its basic needs is not a sovereign nation but a sovereign market.

"Destroy these fiscal paradises and in three days I will rebuild this nation."

It is not good for a nation to have all resources, else its citizens would be lazy and less intuitive by self-sufficiency. It is not good for a nation to lack all resources else its citizens would be wild and greedy.

Although the State wholly belongs to its people, we are never sure that its people wholly belong to the State. That is why in any case the rule of law should be considered paramount over its people.

Progress is not a wish designed in cosmetic slogans or aesthetics in romantic eloquence. It is the rough confrontation of facts, even in silence, characterized by daring, sacrifice, hard work, smart work, strategic outfit crowned with responsibility, accountability, and governance.

Mixing State and religion brings disorder. Separating them completely brings chaos.

National doxology:

> United States: "God bless America."
>
> United Kingdom: "God bless our queen."
>
> Russia: "God bless our Government."
>
> Is.ra.el: "God bless our land."
>
> Iran: "Allah bless our *Ayatollah*."
>
> Perpetual rulers: "long live the president. Thanks Mr. President."

Reduce military by 75% but increase capabilities by 25%, increase cooperation expertise by 25% and step up governance by 25%, and this nation would be more dangerous than a hundred thermo-nuclear bombs.

There is no great nation without a dirty past. There is no small nation without a great future.

COURAGE

Never be afraid to disagree because if you unjustly agree, it would inevitably lead to greater disagreement.

It is better to strive fearlessly and succeed late than to enjoy throughout in mediocrity in the arms of your opponent.

Every inspiration starts as a sort of absurdity/obscurity, which upon insistence and persistence clarifies itself. Those who cling only to clarity can hardly appreciate inspiration because it is the ability to persevere continuously for dark clouds to progressively disappear.

Only those who refuse to start all over again accept the verdict of doom as they surrender the call to greatness.

The first reward we get from perseverance in good action is criticism. When we persevere against criticism we get encouragements. When we persevere through encouragements we get congratulations.

Perseverance is also stubbornness. To be good, one must be stubborn, in the right sense.

All starts with a dream, but too much dream kills the dream.

Never give up. Never take down.

There is an opportunity in every obscurity. We only need the torch of courage to spot the possibility.

CORRECTED SAYINGS

There is time for everything. A time to tell people that *all is vanity* and a time to tell them that *all is not vanity; that* life is a treasure trove.

Every road leads to roam. Every roam leads to Rome.

Behind every successful man is a woman; in front of every unsuccessful man is a woman.

Man is a means to man, "not a wolf to man."

CREATION

Many think that creation evolved while others believe that it was designed. But knowing that Evolution Theory is a *design* and that Design Theory evolves, we come to the conclusion that creation is a Design Evolution.

DEATH

The fear of death often causes the death of fear.

Battling fearlessly to death for a just cause is better than living freely in the hands of your enemy.

Death is an opportunity for those who rightly wait for it. It is a misfortune for those who hang to life in the wrong way.

Death is a faithful friend while life is an unfaithful one.

Think piously of the day of your death, because there is no evidence that others would do so, no matter the effervescence on their lips.

We live because of life. We die because of death.

We live for death and we, unwontedly, die for life.

DESTINY AND FATE

Hazard is an unexpected necessity, while necessity is an expected hazard.

Hazard does not occur by hazard, chance does not occur by chance, necessity does not occur by necessity.

We cannot say with certitude whether things happen for a reason; however, we are certain that we can make or find a purpose in everything that happens.

In divine engineering, there are no hazards or accidents, only unskillful agents who don't know how to fit the parts together.

Fate is when circumstances triumph over hard work, sacrifice, and love. Destiny is when wishes, love, and hard work triumph over circumstances.

Do not force nor forge, for in these simple encounters and counters are designed the glorious paths of destiny.

If you surrender goodwill and justice for a favor, then you have surrendered destiny in exchange for fate.

Where there is determination there is no determinism, and *vice versa*.

ECONOMY-BUSINESS

The politics of this economy must change if the economy has to change society.

They spent time fixing the economy, but the economy remains *fixed*. Friend, create your own game and be master of it before you are eliminated or accused to be the cause of the problem. We have gone over this several times.

Globalization is the centralization of resources marked by the decentralization of scarcity. Both strategically kept apart by a consensus called cooperation.

Communism is simply capitalism at a national scale. Capitalism is a form of communism at a minor scale. In reality, ideologies do not sufficiently protect the person as they claim, except when they give the person the possibility of protecting himself.

Capitalism is not just an ideology where we vainly accuse a few investors. It is a style of life – characteristic of modern man – where those who have are venerated while those who have least are despised. And woe to those who have nothing because even law or love would find it difficult to rescue them.

Since the beginning, humans have made progress in three different phases with regard to control of the world. The first is through the domestication of nature, the second through the domestication of animals, and the third is through the domestication of man by man. The first is done through work, the second through intelligence, and the third is done through capitalism.

When capitalism becomes paramount, morality becomes the by-product of the capital.

We don't suffer from financial crisis, we suffer from management crisis.

Bankers don't save our money. We save the bankers' money.

Globalization: is it about making a global village or about making a *village* global?

Every human interaction can be described summarily and understood in one question: what is being sold and how is it being bought? Or in one word: business.

The real problem is not the economy but how to economize.

National competitive advantage is not measured only by what we relatively gain from others but most importantly by what we risk by depending on others.

Nations that are good in business are those that have succeeded to create a national attractive brand through which any of its products is seen, and appreciated, and by which unconscious relations are established even if the reality *might* be different.

> **America**: Freedom
>
> **Switzerland**: Safety
>
> **Britain**: Justice
>
> **Germany**: Strength
>
> **China**: Simplification
>
> **Japan**: Efficiency
>
> **Is.ra.el**: Favor

The economy is simply above economics.

Real profitability is not measured only by numerical gain but by sustainability and digital gain.

I.M.F. or I.B.F.? International Monetary Fund or International Bankruptcy Fund?

The major problem is not Wall Street. It is Street Walls [boundary separating the rich and the poor].

Either you do business or you are done by business. There is no way out.

EDUCATION

A certificate certifies the ability to compete for a position while talent certifies the ability of a competence to flourish. So joblessness is for the certificate and not for the talent, which is normal.

How do we consider knowledge?
In America, it is a right.
In England, it is an honor.
In France, it is pride.
In Germany, it is a duty.
In Japan, it is a refuge.
In China, it is a secret.
In Africa, it is a privilege.
In Russia, it is a defense.
In Is.ra.el, it is a gift.

The virtue of knowledge is better than the knowledge of virtue.

Most of what we study today often suffers from an epistemological and cultural bias because for each study we need a reference point, and we often choose the reference point that suits us, our object, our method, and our purpose.

Knowledge, = *know − edge*. Knowledge means knowing the edges, frontiers.

Knowledge is not power, it is authority.

Knowledge without know-how is paralytic
Know-how without knowledge is epileptic.

Knowledge comes from below. Wisdom comes from above.

If you want to empower people, educate them. But when education is not good, it becomes a weapon waged against them, destroying them slowly, and making them weak and defenseless at the mercy of their enemies.

Talent is man-made. Genius is God-made.

It is easy to learn the things that we like and difficult to learn those that we don't like. Disciplining our tastes is the royal path to knowledge.

We study either for ourselves [job for the family], or for our friends [importance for community] or for our nation [progress of the world]. Purpose determines outcome.

Everything we study has a politico-policy impact, and unless we appreciate this impact to its just value, our studies would be of little benefit, and perhaps can be a silent danger against our own welfare and wellbeing.

Everyone can be a genius of his own talent.

Inspiration is not a token that falls haphazardly, even on the lazy and ignorant. It is a reward for the hard working, most daring, and most serious.

Let our teachers not only be among the best and skillful in pedagogy, but also the most passionate and dedicated if we need to transform this generation of distracted young people into a fruitful wave of change.

There are no big talents, inspirations, or ideas. There are only big ways in exploring little talents, inspirations, and ideas.

Anyone who claims to be an intellectual often behaves like a paranoid in hysteric popular display.

The greatest thing you can learn from another is the ability to learn by yourself. The best development you can get from the other is to be able to develop your own potentials.

Do not study like a pious believer who is waiting to be saved by some mysterious rites. Study like a soldier at war, determined to conquer knowledge. If you don't conquer knowledge, you will be conquered by ignorance.

Our teachers must never lose patience in the exercise of their duties for this always leads to a pedagogical miscarriage.

The best teacher is not he who is always strong, but he who is capable of transforming strengths and weaknesses into a pedagogical triumph for the benefit of the student.

Because your mind had never declared its retirement to learn, you become an insult and a shame to your own mind.

Education that does not lead to a positive transformation of the individual and his environment certainly leads to his vulnerability, destitution, and destruction.

It is virtue to learn from others and a vice to always lean on them.

Pedagogy evolves through four phases:

i. Master teaches student.

ii. Master guides student to instruct himself.

iii. Master dialogues with student in mutual progressive instruction.

iv. Master delimits the boundary of instruction.

Pedagogy is not simply 'extract from' as it is said in its etymological origin.

Knowledge manifests itself in four stages :

i. Information or an idea.

ii. Message – using information to discover the meaning of things. iii. Transformation – using message to transform a

situation

iv. Power – using transformation to get control of things, people and institutions.

ENDURANCE

He who goes farther even when tired kills tiredness.

With all sincerity, fear those who praise you. With all determination, be reserved towards those who criticize you. With all your strength, never cease to move fearlessly towards the good and the just.

Never say the battle has begun until the opponent starts to shed blood. Never say the battle is over until you have shed your last blood. Battling in life is a trick of courage and perseverance.

ENEMY

Moving defenselessly silent towards the truth, with the defenseless shield of silent truth, the enemy becomes his most feared enemy because he is his most hated enemy.

Enemy at the door: Disarm
   him with truth,
   Extinguish him with charity,
   Destroy him with love,
   Paralyze   him   with affection,
   Blind him with silence,
   and he would be a lasting
   ally.

Never be dependent on your enemy for anything, even on his anger. On the contrary, let him be dependent on you, even on your silence. And as he gradually diminishes to his lowest factor, he would openly admit, without shame, his imminent defeat.

Every innocent blood always revenges itself without shedding blood. Every innocently accused revenges without criminally accusing. Virtue is more *dangerous* than vice.

Non-violence is the appropriate way to extinguish the enemy because it is, indeed, a psycho-emotional attack more violent than the physical which destroys the enemy at his very core and ore, leaving him helpless with all his arms. So nonviolence is not a defenseless defense, but an offense-less offense.

In most cases, the enemy from without is a strategic fabric technically designed to fight the real enemy from within. Prudence, the real destruction, which is imminent, shall come from within, and the supposed enemy would not only emerge innocent but also as the helper and friend.

Never allow your enemies to agree among each other, otherwise, your downfall would be imminent.

Never criticize your enemy in public. He might be saying something good about you and praying for your forgiveness.

In most cases, the supposed enemy is simply a friend of the third class whom we reconsider only when our most preferential friends are absent.

If only the enemy knew how much we love him, this issue would be over.

If we knew how much the enemy loves us, we would call this issue over.

Indeed, there are no real enemies but only real misunderstandings.   Misunderstandings are simply about diverse interests.

The more the enemy is hated, the more he is radicalized. The more he is loved the more he becomes an ally. Now, if the problem with the enemy is our relation with him, then it is not wrong to affirm that we are the real enemy.

The best way to defend yourself from the enemy is to make him an ally.

Unless the enemy becomes a friend, our virtue remains suspicious.

Each time you triumph over anger, fear, laziness, and ignorance, your enemy feels very disappointed.

Tell the enemy that we are not dead and that we have forgiven him, and simply request that he lays down his arms and changes his ways.

Surrender! Because it is time to make peace, any headiness would turn your war against you.

ENVY

Envy not the poor, they never choose to be what they are.

Envy not the rich, they often choose to be what they are not.

It is a crime to refuse to be oneself, evil to wish to be another.

EVIL

When men do wrong shamelessly, they often compensate for it by doing good where and when it is not supposed to be done and to whom it is least needed. Vain is this gain.

Selfishness is the prison in which we lock ourselves as a retribution or vengeance for our inability to set ourselves free through the love of others.

Every evil has a casualty that is proportional to the momentum of the evil act. Every good has a by-product which is proportional to the impact of the good deed.

It is difficult to suspect others without being suspicious of our suspicion.

Men's desire to do evil is often fulfilled when a little wrong is done unto them so that they can use it is a justification to accomplish what they really intended.

Sin is not diminished by religious effervescence.

The triumph of evil in our society has evolved in three phases following the direction of our main story lines. The first phase was the fight of good against evil where the good always won.

The second phase was the fight of evil against good where evil or lesser evil often   won.

The third phase is our modern age where evil fights evil and it is the greater evil that often triumphs.

We have prepared the path for our own eschatology.

It is often out of selfishness that we complain about the selfishness of others.

The revenge of evil is that it always falls without being attacked.

Selfishness is a sign of boredom and frustration.

When there is democratization of error and evil, the just become those who integrate stubbornness as a new paradigm of life.

The best way to show that we hate others is to forbid them from being themselves.

False: Either the wrong is said for the right reason, or the right is said for the wrong reason. It is still false!

Dishonesty: a truth is used to defend a lie and a lie used to defend a truth. In either case, it is a lie.

FAILURE

The greatest error is the inability to detect error.

Everyone who fails always has an excuse, and unless you conquer your excuses you shall make no change or progress.

Success is either what we gain as benefit or what we avoid as deficit. Failure is seeing things only in one direction.

FAITH AND REASON

Faith and Reason:

In reality, faith is a concept that designates a state or nature of the capacitation of properties of reason enabling it to appreciate things in a given way or identify certain unidentified realities. Because reason can exist without faith while faith cannot exist without reason, it therefore follows that faith – which comes by hearing and accepted by reason – is in itself reason with a double function that comes into exercise depending on its level of capacitation. Reason is like a radar that detects and appreciates realities depending on its designed capabilities and the way it is digitized in exercise. The classical distinction between faith and reason is based on the false assumption that faith is an entity in itself that can be juxtaposed with, and has led to 10 centuries [Middle Age] of fruitless theologicophilosophical debate which recently culminated in the parallel analogy of *Fides et Ratio* of great J.P. II as two wings of a bird that enables it to fly.

Faith is belief in what we don't see; hope is aspiration in what we don't see. We cannot hope without faith and we cannot have faith without hope. They are two sides of the same coin, held by love.

Belief is the knowledge of not knowing. The knowledge of not knowing is not ignorance because it postulates a being in order to rationalize being in existence.

Reason is above faith: practically and theoretically.

FAMILY

The family is the main place of real refuge, security and peace for everyone. Any other human grouping offers multiple alternatives but also with multiplied possibilities of violence characteristic of its constitutive fabric – interest.

By procreation a person sees how strong a human can be. After birth the person becomes a witness of how powerless he or she can be.

There is no perfect way to bring up a child because those who bring them up are not perfect and their circumstances are less ideal. However, we know that non-ideal persons can offer ideal love which would serve as an ideal opportunity to bring out the best of him and his environment.

In theory, the head of the family is love. In practice, the head of the family is money.

When the family becomes dangerous the individual loses love.
When society becomes dangerous the individual loses freedom.
When the nation becomes dangerous the individual loses hope.

It is noble for children to learn from elders. But when elders stray, it becomes nobler for them to learn from children.

Our children, even when silent, always have a hard judgment on us, for they know that besides all we give and say, our behaviors always betray and weigh greater on them than any other thing.

We can give a child a body not a soul;
Education not wisdom;
A partner not a lover;
Wealth not peace;
Opportunities not success.

The family gives the character, the school gives the knowledge, the society gives the belief, life gives the opportunity, and the individual gives himself his value, but the State collects the taxes.

Bringing up a child is not just a duty to be performed, but a profession to be learned and a vocation for which the parent must dedicate his whole effort, strength, and will.

The main reason why the education of our children often fails is because we care only about our own children. How can our children be good when the multiple of others are not?

Put feminism in society and opposing parts would start to dialogue.

Put feminism in the family and dialoguing parts would start to oppose and break.

Change the women and the nation would change. The progress of women makes the progress of the nation.

Fatherless children do not exist. Because every child has and deserves a father, the father must become one and remain so, technically or financially. Bound by conscience and law to work for each child, this nation shall know greater prosperity.

FOOLISHNESS

Ignorance is the nakedness of the brain. Wherever you are and whatever you do, you would be decoded and mocked.

Only fools never make errors because their whole life is an error.

Giving knowledge to a fool only adds to his foolishness. Unless he corrects his foolishness with wisdom, no knowledge would make him better.

Do not be a genius of your own foolishness. Better be a fool of your own genius.

Never refuse forgiveness when asked. It is not only a sign of acceptance of the other but a sign of acceptance of yourself.

A person who does not know the value of what he has, creates a complicity to his own extinction. A nation that does not valorize what it has, creates a national conspiracy against its own existence.

Mediocrity is the art of starting tomorrow.

Foolishness is a school of thought where the adepts believe that they know everything.

Ignorance:
We know so much about ourselves but nothing about others. We know so much about others but very little about ourselves.
We know very little about ourselves and very little about others.
The first is shameful, the second is a disgrace, and the third is a pity.

Your ignorance is the comfort zone of others.

It is stupid to believe that we must say something about what we know and see, and foolish to believe that we know what is best for others.

FORGIVENESS

Wounds of the flesh bleed blood that can be healed in the hospital. Wounds of the mind bleed ignorance which can be healed with wisdom. Wounds of the heart bleed hatred which can be healed with forgiveness.

If you are capable of *liking*, it means you are capable of love. If you are capable of love it means you are capable of forgiveness. If you are capable to forgive, it means you are capable to forget. Refusal to embrace the cycle of virtues is simply because we choose the virtues that suit our sentiments.

We do not forgive the enemy because we are virtuous or because we want to be virtuous. Indeed, we forgive simply because we admit that we are not virtuous and because we want the enemy to be virtuous.

Forgiveness is the only injustice that is permitted by law.

FREEDOM

This is freedom:

> Free to unite not free to divide;
>
> Free to have rights not free to abuse rights;
>
> Free to enjoy, not free to destroy;
>
> Free to cooperate, not free to separate;
>
> Free to progress, not free to oppress;
>
> Free to gather, not free to scatter;
>
> Free to explore, not free to exploit;
>
> Free to dare, not free to scare;
>
> Free to save, not free to kill;
>
> Free to do justice, not free to exercise injustice;
>
> Free to be free at will, not free to referee at will.

Freedom is the deployment of the will in search for the common well-being, while well-being is the deliberation of self in conformity with the will.

Freedom is the maximum rationalization of laws in a given territory where the will and well-being are submitted (willingly or not) for sanction and protection in a sustainable pattern for maximum security.

Most people fight for their rites instead of fighting for their rights.

Freedom is directly proportional to the law.

What does modern man really mean when he says he is fighting for his rights? He means he wants to be able to possess and dispose of his rights when he wants, where he wants, the way he wants, and with whom he wants. Once more, the battle is lost when rights are possessed and disposed at will.

Those who fight for their freedom always know how to respect it and be truly free. Those who receive it freely often know how to abuse it and be imprisoned by it.

There must not be a law for everything. Where the law does not intervene directly/indirectly is the privileged territory of freedom.

We derive our freedom not by virtue of our personal existence but by virtue of the existence of the other. Not because the other gives us freedom but because his freedom justifies our freedom and his lack of freedom is an imminent threat to our supposed freedom.

In reality, love sets us free while truth sets love free.

To be free, we must accept that nothing is free. Thus freedom is the ability to pay our dues duly and justly.

Any freedom that is not fought for is always lived as a debt – which is paid later.

Freedom is the attachment to just laws. Lack of freedom is bondage in unjust laws. Therefore freedom is the law.

There is a fee for everything free.

Freedom is not liberty and liberty is not freedom. Freedom is the nature and disposition to be or do what one wants. Liberty is the exercise of freedom in being or doing what one wants.

Always choose what you want in life. Failure to do so would make you the object of the choices of others. And what they choose for you would often not be the best.

Prisoners are in constant search for freedom. Free people are in constant fear of losing their freedom. They are related, we simply react differently to our un-free conditions.

The limit of freedom is freedom. That is, freedom limits freedom.

Freedom is a process not a possession.

FRIENDSHIP

Being together is always at the cost of refusing to be oneself. Succeeding together is the means by which we become our true selves.

Make good relations not only with friends but also with solitude, for one thing is certain: no matter how faithful they are, they won't be with you all the time – solitude would remain your refuge.

Only those who consider friends as liable opponents and opponents as liable allies would not be disappointed in this life.

Friendship is a means by which we accept our true selves and the end for which others are accepted for their true selves.

A true friend would show you and lead you through the path of success.
A close person would kindly show you the right way.

Friendship

      F= Fidelity

      R= Respect

      I= Interaction
      E= Encouragement

N= Negotiate

D= Discipline

S= Simplicity

H= Hospitality

I= Inspire

P= Perseverance

A bad friend would prefer to give you food, drinks, and drugs in order to distract you from your goal. Please, for love of yourself, stop drinking with him.

Rely on friends to the extent to which they are reliable.

Friends are mirrors through which we see ourselves.
When they are bad, they make us see ourselves as always good.
When they are good, they make us see our imperfections.

What do our so-called friends say about us in our absence? And what do our so-called enemies say about us in our absence? Almost the same thing.

Friends are made, they are not natural. Enemies are made, they are not natural. Our ability to choose has made us dangerous to ourselves and others.

Losing a good friend is like losing part of your vocabulary, making us ineffective in expressing ourselves. That is why we search for synonyms, but like all other synonyms they never replace the missing word completely.

Most people don't have friends, but allies.

Friendship is mutual tolerance versus mutual censor in a sustainable pattern called respect.

Never seek to conserve friends for others need them too and might be more caring towards them than we are. It is bad to be greedy about friends.

Love of friend and love of enemy are similar: they both yield the same impact – love.

There are no perfect friends, only perfect allies.

Friendship is the summit of all virtues. A summit without summit.

It is unfriendly to wish everyone to be your friend. It is against friendship to want everybody you choose as friend to indeed be your friend.

Do not be anxious in having too many friends. It always leads to a relational constipation.

It is unfriendly to expect too much from a friend.

When a friend becomes an enemy, we become vulnerable twice and he becomes dangerous twice.

If you have learnt nothing from your friend, then your friend needs to learn something from you. If not, both of you agree because you acknowledge your mutual uselessness.

FUN AND MEANING

Politicians don't tell lies. Politicians simply lay the truth but don't lie. A lie is a disorientation of goodwill against the good, but politics is not strictly about *goodwill* but the orientation of public thoughts towards right action. Public thoughts are not imputable morally though they are adjudicated legally.

Those who desired to get something or someone but lacked the real purchasing power decided to technically create the word love in order to facilitate their cause, thus giving such a word all the exceptional qualities that their purchasing power couldn't afford.

Today, people borrow not only money. They also borrow love, marriage, and friendship. When paying back, do not forget the interest rates.

What job do you want?
Politician: You'll be on public persecution where every effort would be criticized and considered suspicious.
Teacher: You'll teach people who would be greater than you, and would hardly think of you.
Player (soccer): You'll become a public instrument for popular amusement.

Artist: You'll be tossed here and there at the mercy of unpredictable fans that command you.

Priest/pastor: You'll be venerated for who you are not, making you to appear to be what you are not and say what you are unable to accomplish.

Doctor: You'll be a steward to pharmaceutical enterprises and friend to diseases.

Pilot/Driver: You'll spend your time transporting people who have important things to do, certainly because you got none.

Journalist: You'll always tell people's stories and share their ideas but your own story would be neglected because it is assumed that you've got none.

Banker: You'll live on people's money and labor and repaying them with greater financial crisis.

Diplomat: Flattery, warfare without arms.

Engineer: You'll toil to fuel the vanity of men with multiple products and later be accused of technical defaults and ecological mischief.

Thinker: The peaceful rider with no salary, no employer, but never jobless, always thinking.

God created the world in seven days

God said: 'Let there be Light' and there was Intelligence. Seeing that all was good, He said again: 'Let there be Beauty' and there was Truth. And in truth, He said: 'Let there be work' and there was success. Success was delightful to Him and He said in delight: 'Let there be virtue' and there was Happiness. Happily He said: 'Let there be Gentleness and there was Peace. Peacefully He said: 'Let there be man'. And man said it is not enough. When God added woman, they both said: 'your job is done, let us continue from here.' God saw that all was beautiful and blessed them with grace and freedom; after that, He went to His dwelling on high.

GOODNESS

We want all the good things on our side, to whom shall the bad ones go? The only sustainable good is the common good.

The common good is not the sum of each individual welfare. It is the surplus from each individual good from which each person derives sustainable satisfaction.

Evil people equally enjoy the good things that good people aspire for. The main advantage of being good is that it is sustainable. Goodness is sustainability.

If you can be good, you can be better. If you can become better, you definitely can be best.

Not every good act is good. If a good done to the other makes him more dependent on the doer it becomes a strategic violence, suffering from virtue deficiency syndrome. Every good must weigh its sustainable impact.

Give only what belongs to you and take only what you deserve. Those who like to give what does not belong to them often take what does not belong to them.

Predicting what will happen has nothing to do with God's will, else the will of God will be the product of the fabrication of a coherence confirmed by reality.

Nor the inability to predict means incapacity of doing God's will. The will of God is the will of God and the will of man is the will of man, though both can meet at a common point called goodness.

Does God love the good we do in itself or He loves the idea that such good is being done in His name? Strictly speaking, the name of God is the Good, so doing good is spelling His name practically. Our God is a practical God, not a concept to be flattered by the caress of romantic thoughts.

The most sacred rite is right.

Making one heart at a time happy and loving can change a society more than addressing eloquent speeches to several people at a time.

Does man need God to be good? If yes, then every atheist is fundamentally bad and every believer necessarily good. If no, then virtue is a human quality inherent in man for which he must live to, irrespective of his belief. Belief is a metaphysical framework which enables him operationalize what is human in him.

In principle, we are not as good as we think. We are not as bad as others think.

GOD

God is not the uncaused cause. He is an uncaused effect.

If God had a nationality, many would think He is either from Rome, Jerusalem, or Saudi Arabia. But perhaps He seems to be from Tibet, still struggling to get his independence from the dominant convictions of men.

The best escape is where there is no escape.

The greatest enemies of God are those who believe that God needs their permission and collaboration in order to accomplish His mission on earth.

The God-argument always follows the *sum-all-principle* where every explanation and counter explanation are matched to a fact and expected to sum up to the conclusion that is desired.

If God does not play dice, then He plays chess. If He plays the dice then He is unjust. If He plays chess, then He is a politician.

God is not an idea *of* man, he is an idea *in* man.

God prefers an atheist who loves and shows mercy to a religious person who is selfish, wicked, and dishonest.

God is the answer for those who have the right question.
He is the question for those who have the wrong answer.

If God exists, why is he hiding from us?
If man exists why is he hiding himself from God?
We think wrongly because we ask the wrong questions.

God is not the beginning and the end. God is the *unbegan* beginning and the unending end.

We need God because we are needy. We love God because He is lovely.

God answers those who answer Him.

The easiest way to be far from God is to believe that He is only on our side.

Never give up loving God, for God has never given up loving you, and showing you His mercy.

The God of love commands love of God.

God is the only lonely being that does not experience loneliness, the only friendly being that does not need friendship.

Admitting the existence of God is reasonable. Admitting His non-existence is rationality.

Instead of searching for God, they search for the God particle.

Do not believe in the God of a person who hates you.

When man refuses to do what is his for himself, God also refuses to do what is His for him.

Who has man been to God? A disgrace.
Who has God been to man? A disappointment.
Who has man been to himself? A liar.
Who has God been to himself? A gambler.

GOVERNANCE, POLICY

Governance is the harmonious coordination of matrices of the economy of sociopolitical dynamics following the quadruple principle of participation (*political*), accountability (*economical*), sustainability (*human*) and transparency (*legal*).

Governance is above politics. Politics is a means to an end.

Governance is a means and its own end.

There is no ideal solution to (public) policy problems, there are only ideal characteristics: continuity, sustainability, optimality, punctuality, generality in specificity, simplicity, comprehensibility, compressibility, applicability, acceptability, adaptability, and accessibility.

Public policy is the instrumental stronghold of governance.

Governance is the operational essence of public policy.

'Governance, to whom shall we go? You have the key to perpetual growth.'

GAME

Sports is governed by deontology not morality, although deontology is inspired by morality

Playing by the rules means playing around the rules – politics.

Playing by the rules means playing the rule – economy.

Playing by the rules means being played by the rule – society.

Play no game without mastering the rules. How do we master the rules without playing the game?

In every game there is a trick. No matter how much you know about the game if you don't master the trick, you will always be the loser.

GREATITUTES

Great are those who are not great or who dream not to be great. On them reposes all greatness.

Great are those who have fallen a thousand times and are laughed at, because at the lowest ebb, they can't fall again- only glory awaits them.

Great are those who are misunderstood. They shall learn to understand better.

Great are the frustrated, those who have nothing. They have nothing to lose and nothing to fear again.

Great are the wise, for they know their weaknesses.

Great are those who are insulted, or neglected. They will learn to count on themselves, and thus become strong and courageous.

Great are the abandoned. They will make a safe home of rest for the mind.

Great are the simple and truthful, the kingdom of peace is theirs.

Great are those who are judged, dismissed or sent to prison, only such know what is real justice and who is really just.

HAPPINESS

We can be happy only to a certain extent. Beyond that point, we become delirious.

If the quest for happiness makes you subject to persistent injustice and violence, then it is better to choose unhappiness. The truth is that unhappiness is not a vice in any way. Tolerating injustice as a means to happiness is great vice.

Happy is the man who stops seeking happiness. Being at equilibrium —or at peace,- he would be sought by happiness.

Pleasure is the quantity of life. Happiness is the quality of life while love is the quality of happiness.

In reality, happiness is not a possession of something. It is rather the value attributed to a possession.

Happiness is transmittable, but pleasure is not. That is why those who are happy are treasures for others. Suffering is contagious, but pain is not. That is why those who suffer often affect others greatly.

Happiness is simply pleasure at the right place, time and reason. Happiness is also suffering at the right place for the right reason.

Peace is the legacy of justice.
Happiness is the legacy of love.

It is difficult for a fool to be really happy. Happiness is understanding the limits of happiness.

Satisfaction is when desires are met. Despair is when desires are not met. Happiness is when desires are not desired.

Only those who readily accept not to be fulfilled reach fulfillment in life.

It is not good for man to be completely happy.

HISTORY

Witnessing history as an idle spectator is being absent from it altogether.

Knowing the truth but refusing to say it means living an existential lie.

Failing to defend a just cause means defending the wrong one that you dislike.

Being indifferent in a paradox means taking sides against your own interest.

History gives to each people their own challenges and difficulties where it remains wholly to them to rise and get the solution. It sanctions gravely the refusal to confront its challenges. There is no way out. What we cover privately and technically is always uncovered publicly and strategically, because flying away from a problem only takes us deeper into the problem itself.

History is rational. If this is not corrected, it would repeat itself.

The only thing that is constant in historic dynamics is change.

Crimes in history can never be appropriately repaid. The best way is usually to pledge solemnly that such crimes will never be committed again technically, strategically, symbolically, and spiritually. Reparation is properly done by restoration of the future not by mending the past.

Men make history while history makes men.

Life is fashioned by fate and destiny. History is designed by determination and opportunity.

The history of humanity is divided into three phases: the first when he didn't know what to do; the second when he came to the understanding of the right thing to do; the third, when he would be transformed into the good thing he knows.

When people corrupt history, history corrupts them.

History is fluid not brut,
dynamic not static,
cyclical not lineal,   a
process not a possession,
procedural not a produce,
human not superhuman,
rational not rationalistic.
multi-polar not unipolar,
man-made not man.

HONESTY AND INTEGRITY

A corrupt business man is a traitor to his partner; he is unworthy of confidence. A corrupt politician is a traitor to all citizens and his nation; he is unworthy of trust and a disgrace to the nation. A corrupt religious person is a traitor to himself, to all believers, and to God; he is a shame to humanity.

Those who flatter always get flattery for their paycheck. And, flatter no one for whatever favor, because others would flatter you to get the same favors back.

HUMILITY, SIMPLICITY

We would never have enough until we refuse to have enough.

Falling in love with self is bad. Self-hate is evil. Self-neglect is suicidal.

Who has ever had all he wanted except he who never desired to get all he wanted?

Greatness empties us while simplicity fulfills us.

The praise we receive from others corrupts. The desire for such praise is corruption in itself.

What we like is not necessarily what we deserve. What we deserve is not necessary what we like. Humility is the ability to accept these contradictions. Wisdom enables us to know the difference.

Humility is pride in the right place and time.

In fact, every man has a talent; at least, the good sense of acknowledging the talent of others, and being at their service.

Humility is the arrogance of the brave and the wise.

If a humble man should be crushed to pieces because he is humble, then it is better to choose pride and resist mercilessness and humiliation. Humility is pride for the just cause.

Never have a modest opinion of your accomplishments when you merit them, but always have a modest opinion about yourself, for you do not merit your own being.

Modest things often yield great joy and happiness while extravagant things often yield modest joy and great worries.

Calm down. Never boast that you are an intellectual. This always leads to a personality disorder.

Anyone who strives to get everything right through "rights" always does so at the cost of doing wrong.

"I am different from others." This is what you'll always hear from those who behave like all others.

HUMANITY, MAN

In the kingdom of humanity, *Reason* is the king, *Love* is the queen, *Truth* is the prince and *Kindness* is the princess. The servants are Justice, Peace, Humility, Prudence, Tolerance, Hard Work, Forgiveness and Discipline. Out of this kingdom we cease to be humans.

Where a person comes from defines him technically. Where he is going defines him strategically. Where he is defines him structurally. Where he dies defines him existentially.

What is modern man? He is emotionally dissipative, religiously a believer, politically a democrat, economically a capitalist, socially individualistic, culturally transversal, morally secular, intellectually systemic and systematic. In fact, a combination of everything that makes him undoubtedly attractive yet unpredictably dangerous, like a ballistic missile.

Who are we?
Battling courageously to survive in life through deterrence and daring – soldiers.
Striving to establish balance and harmony in diversified social connections – politicians.

Inventors of numerous social matrices which are constantly repaired, renovated, and polished – engineers.
Zealots of truth where we offer sacrifices of charity and love – priests.
Investors in inter-actions or cont-acts while leaning where we get maximum interest – businessmen. Actors in scenes we didn't choose and spectators in scenes where we can conveniently choose – comedians.
Subjects in a world we didn't create and objects in the world where we are creators – adventurers.

What does modern man really want? Surely, he wants *wants* only!

Man is not the measure of all things. The measure of all things is man. The first is the objective case and is relative.
The second is the nominative case which is absolute.

The singularity of individuality makes sense only in the plurality of humanity. The two are symmetrically related though asymmetrically constituted. Man is an individual plurality while humanity is a plural singularity.

What are we talking about? Feminity, feministics or feminism? The first is the dynamic mobility of the feminine nature; the second is the study of the feminine nature while the third is the ideology of the feminine.

Man is tired of fellow man because he is tired of being man.

We belong to humanity, but humanity does not belong to us.

No one chooses freely his own individuality or singularity. Because we do not possess the code for our individuality, we cannot, in any way, disprove that the other is just another form of our own individuality for whom respect is just a sign for the respect of our own individuality. What differs is the consciousness of each individuality.

Fundamentally, people don't change from who they are. They simply change the way they react to their unchanging nature.

We have had all the things of desire. But why do we continue to desire?
We have never had the things we desire, why don't we stop desiring?
Man is defined by his desire, and desire is the desire for desire.

We have been caught red-handed or duped by our own flesh because escape from it is an apology of guilt. Succumbing to it is the eschatology of guilt.

It is not good for man to be perfect. It is not good for man not to wish perfection.

Humans have not changed. They have simply changed the way they acquire their unchanged interests.

To each individual, life gives its own challenges and opportunities discriminately but with indiscriminate potentials of forging a destiny of happiness and peace through the dynamic evolution of the will.

To be human is to be humane.

IDEAS

The universal is not a *particular* with ideal characteristics that claims to be universal (this is imperial), nor the sum of *particulars* harmonized to be universal (this is collegial). The universal is rather the summit beyond each ideal *particular* from which various *particulars* derive their singular idealization (this is referential) as a means of appreciation of the ideal universal (this is inferential) – stating the imperative of dialogue.

There are no ideal ideologies, only ideal patterns of applying ideologies, which are never ideal in themselves.

Creativity is arithmetically limited but geometrically unlimited.

Everything is on earth including God. Nothing is in heaven except God. I don't know why people complain so much about earth and are too excited about heaven.

Some die for the ideal while others die for the idea. But these make little sense. I prefer that the ideal and the idea should die for the sake of humans. Only in this way shall humans be able to rebuild the ideal and the idea that would sustain humanity.

INTELLIGENCE/KNOWLEDGE

The abundance of information to numerous people through all means has only made real intellectuals too scarce to find.

Intelligence does not designate a reality in itself. Rather, it is simply a concept designating the capability of an individual to mobilize the faculties of the brain (memory:30%, reasoning:30%, will:30% and imagination, intuition, emotion etc:10%) in attaining implicit or explicit goals within a defined space of time.

Those who reach the top of education are not necessarily the most intelligent but the most persevering. In fact, intelligence is not only a knowing potential, it is also a human quality.

There are three stages in memory in the creation of intelligence:
Primary memory: - Registers basic categories of things: numbers, letters, shapes and figures.
Secondary memory: - Registers basic concepts: God, man, plans, lives, animals, etc.
Tertiary memory: - Registers basic ideas/things: in mathematics, individual shapes and names.

INNOCENCE

It is self-defilement inflicted on oneself when we skillfully transfer the evil we do to innocent persons through the medium of designed accusations.

No one who loves gifts can be judged innocent.

Being innocent is extremely costly, but it is worthwhile.

When our love turns to indifference, it means we have done injustice to ourselves. When our indifference turns to love, it means we have done justice to the other.

JOB AND PROFESSION

Unemployment evolved through three phases:
Firstly, when individuals started accumulating more than they required, thus needing assistance – labor. Secondly, when papers were the measure of some supposed competence – certificates.
Thirdly, when skills had to correspond only to a particular task – specialization.
The first is capitalistic, the second is programmatic, and the third is systematic. Today we suffer from all three.

There is more work than the number of people searching for work. Thus, it is a problem of searching for money, not really work.

Do not only do the job you want. Above all, love the job you do.

There is no job crisis. There is only a creativity crisis.

JUSTICE

Justice is the [un]equal distribution of resources and [un]balanced retribution or attribution of acts in a way that gives highest satisfaction for the maximum or least dissatisfaction for a few.

None of our talents/accomplishments is exclusively a sole merit of ours without an unmerited internal or external disposition contributing a great deal. Because we owe a great deal to these dispositions, we are indisputably indebted towards them and towards others.

That all humans are equal with equal rights is the foundation of all justice. That humans are always unequal with unequal privileges is the summit of all injustice. Justice is an *a priori* idea while injustice is an *a posteriori* fact.

Rights are respected where obligations are honored.

Justice should be applied without sentiments, especially when injustice is done with impunity. It should be withheld with reason when injustice is done with sufficient reason.

Those who fight for justice are those who have practiced injustice, those who have suffered injustice, or those who have experienced both. The first fights by redefining the law, the second fights by disobeying or escaping from the law and the third fights by reinterpreting the law.

It is unjust to seek justice at all cost. Justice should be sought at the price of justice and in a just way.

When we seek to defend our rights to the maximum, we often loss it. To be safe, we must be able to surrender part of our rights to the other in order to rightfully conserve what remains to us.

Injustice is natural. Justice is un-natural.

JOY

Nowadays, the joy of living comes by clinging happily to the things of death: drugs, alcohol, smoking etc. Yet, we claim to flee death through the front door, though embracing it through the back door.

He who is incapable of tears is incapable of joy.

We don't enjoy the present because we always believe that the future would be better. Because the future is often less than expected or not better at all, we often talk of our joys only in the past, even though we ignored those moments when they were present.

Be joyful openheartedly because the days of worries are often much.

Joy that is not shared reduces in intensity and proportion.
When shared it increases in density and propensity.

LANGUAGE

"Zero" doesn't mean "nothingness". It is rather the absence of nothingness or the presence of nothing.

There is only one language that humans understand: *interest*.

The masculinization of language has three causes: lack of creativity, laziness, and strategy. And it has three consequences: imprecision, stagnation, and subordination respectively.

The *realization* of mathematics is based on the *mathematization* of the real. Also, the *realization* of ideas is based on the *idea-lization* of the real. Because ideas and maths are only forms of perceptions of the real, there is consequently no complete compressibility of the *real*.

LAW AND ORDER

A state of law is not so much about the absence of crimes but more about the "professionalization" of crime for the benefit of all through the State of law. Thus no fighting but boxing/wrestling, no cheating/stealing but numerous casinos, no promiscuity but corporate prostitution.

There are three types of criminals: the hot blooded, the warm blooded, and the cold blooded. The first commits crime out of anger for his interest, the second commits crimes for the interest of a few in the name of society, and the third commits crimes for his interest in the name of God. The first is sanctioned by violence from the law, the second is sanctioned by political disintegration from voters, and the third is sanctioned by reverence from believers.

Never be ignorant of the law because the law is not ignorant of you.

The best way to test the justness of a law is to apply it to those who make it.

In criminal justice, self-defense is not alter-offense. Self-defense is valid only in appropriate proportional use of force against unjustified offense, and it can be invalidated if the offended has the evidence of no evidence and if the offender has the evidence of counter evidence. The evidence of no evidence means the offended is defenseless, thus less offensive while the evidence of counter evidence means the offender's evidence suffers the fact of being in the wrong place, time and possession of what he is not duly entitled to. Because the offended is absent – dead, and can't claim justice or suffers incapacity to fair justification, and since the offender is his primary witness in claim for self-defense, his arguments must suffer no evidence of counter evidence and his claim must weigh more than the evidence of counter evidence – because the defunct might have been acting in self-defense but fell short of resources.

Man is a sovereign value and the justness of any law is determined by its ability to promote this value in the best possible way in his community.

It is better to establish penalization of inappropriate acts though leaving them liberal in exercise than to establish depenalization because they are liberal in exercise.

The objective of the law is not only for retribution, approbation or deterrence. It is pedagogic: an education. It is deontological: a code. It is systemic: the soul of social architecture. Technical: a skill and fashion of social architects. It is strategic: an arm deployed justifiably or not against opponents from within and from without.

And ideographic: defines the identity of a people.

Either we choose to have perfect laws and live in a perfectly unjust and evil society, or we choose to have perfectible laws and live in a perfectible just and good society.

A law with no exception is an exception.

Never make so many laws for yourself than you can keep. This would only add to your existing worries and troubles.

"None should be ignorant of the law." This is the best way to restore force to the law even when we know that our lawyers don't know all the laws.

'Dura lex cera lex'. The Law is hard but it is the law. Knowing that in all times, the law has been unable to save the weak and the poor, that it has been more accessible to the smart, rich and strong, and often gambled with, depending on diverse interest rates, it should be said, on the contrary, that the *law is weak but it is the law*, since it often doesn't do what it is expected to do, the way it should be done and for whom it should be justly done.

(Contextually, the law, according to the Romans, was made often exclusively by the upper minority class, and being hard to the lower class, they said it was the law that was hard. In brief, it was a strategy to perpetuate power and bind opponents.)

LAZINESS, IDLENESS

Sleep means passive rest of the conscious mind and passive action of the unconscious mind. That most people are passive in their actions shows that they have spent almost all their life sleeping.

When people gather to talk about you, they would surely attribute to you qualities that you don't have or vices that you have never done.

The error of a lazy and selfish person often leads to catastrophe and danger, while the error of a hardworking and honest person often leads to opportunities and strength.

Those who never accomplish anything substantial are those who always claim to have better and greater ideas, but usually say that they'll start tomorrow.

Laziness is the art of considering work as a burden. Fairness is considering work as a duty. Smartness is considering it as a privilege.

Lazy people are often those who wait to do big things, while hard-working people are those who do little things constantly.

The cost of being lazy is far greater than the cost of hard work and sacrifice.

The laziest animal in the forest is the lion. The most hardworking is the ant. Those whom we fear because of their strength are often lazy and weak while those whom we despise are often strong and useful.

When we let others do for us what we can easily do for ourselves, we become vulnerable and a danger to ourselves.

Laziness is the punishment that we inflict on ourselves when we refuse to get better.

Mediocrity is lowliness with regard to the other. It is violence with regard to oneself.

Screen viewers always take their idleness very seriously: that is the trick; they need to feel that they are very busy.

Lazy people always lack time to do more because they are too busy with idleness. Hard-working people often have time to do more because they feel idle doing less.

LIFE

In this banquet of life, there are numerous delicacies around which we all assemble to feast. The scent gives satisfaction but also hunger as we thirst for life. When we taste, we need more, never satisfied. Moving from one dish to the other gives constipation and dissatisfaction. Some dishes seem better only because they have not been tasted, while others look less tasteful because we are too familiar with them. Those who start eating often retreat and retire first while those who serve others to eat always eat last, but eat the most and are the most satisfied. The worst experience is usually for those who eat the most or those who never participated. And as we feasts, we always forget that the important thing in the feast is not the food or the drinks but the encounter, the celebration of pains and joys.

If a law is unjust for the benefit of the whole community, then it is better than, and should be preferred, to a 'just' law made for the benefit of an individual.

What is the meaning of life? It is the life of meaning.

Life has four cardinal points: To the North, grace giving us light. To the west, reason giving us truth. To the east, talent giving us success. To the south, emotion giving us delight.

Revolving through these points are possibilities and obstacles. Peace, progress, and happiness are sure only when we move at the speed of prudence with the momentum of charity.

It takes vigilance to grasp an opportunity, hard work to grasp a talent, reason to grasp success, passion to grasp gratification, and grace to know the difference.

No life is a merit but simply a credit.

Everything has been said about life except one: it is a silent music, a motionless dance in an empty orchestra where we enjoy in silence to the glory of the only perfect silent musician – God.

The highest good you can do in life is to do good as the highest thing in life.

The dogma of life is to serve life and save life with life for the sake of life.

Life is a circle: it turns round and can go in any direction.
   Love is square: it has opposites and contraries, always.
   Happiness is a triangle: change the sides and one would still point to a specific direction – peace.

Life is like basketball. No matter how expert we are, we can still miss the shot. No matter how amateur we are we can still get it in. The most important thing is to keep shooting.

Life is a struggle between happiness and suffering linked by understanding. The two are difficult to separate because happiness is often characterized by pleasure and pain, while suffering is often characterized by pain and pleasure.

In this life, there is a chance for everybody. If you have no chance, then surely there are others who have accumulated more than they need, including your share. All you need to do is to ask them to give it back using hard work, honesty, creativity, discipline, and integrity.

It is difficult to be alive. It is not easy to die. What do we want?

Listen to no one who says it is over for you. Life knows better how it plays its game.

No life is void of meaning. We are simply unable or unwilling to make meaning out of the meaninglessness of our beings.

Humans are like cards shuffled in the jungle casino of life, where the number of the card matters less but derives all its value from the various combinations made with others. And the type of game being played changes everything because in some games, the dealer is always the winner while in others there are equal or geometric chances to win. Be watchful with the game you play in life because there are many dangerous dealers...

The verdict of being alive is the thirst for more life. That is why we strive, strive and strive. Life is simply striving.

Life is unfair. It is even more unfair when we refuse to admit that it is unfair.

LONELINESS

Friendship is fear of loneliness. Loneliness is often fear of friendship.

A safe loneliness is better to a dangerous relationship, just like dying safely and proudly is better than living dangerously and in shame.

Every loneliness is lived as a failed promise. Every relationship is lived as an imperfect promise.

It is sad not to know what loneliness is, but triumphing over loneliness, we become serene and peaceful.

Knowing loneliness enables us to know the value of friendship.

Another name for loneliness is boredom. Friendship is the fight against boredom.

LOVE

Love is not a favor that we offer to others from the abundance of our loveliness. It is a due that we pay to others for sharing in a humanity we do not own.

To love and to be in love. The first is the just and cheerful kindness consciously offered to all, including the unjust. The second is the unjust and cheerful kindness offered to the one we judge as 'just.'

Love is not a possession. It is a process, or a possession in process, or again a process in possession.

It is insufficient to seek to be loved, but it is more appropriate to give the opportunity and the means to love through love.

MARRIAGE

Stable couples are blended by humility, sacrifice, and dialogue while unstable ones are broken by pride, strength, and theories.

Man and woman can live together by freely choosing not to belong to each other. Husband and wife are together because they choose freely to belong to each other. The first are bonded by their vulnerability to separate while the second are vulnerable to separate by their bonding.

In marriage, one does not surrender freedom to the other, but rather, through a consensus, accepts to share in the freedom of the other. That is, there is authorization to share in another's freedom not authorization over it. It is this possibility to share in the other's freedom that gives us the duty, in the form of a privilege, to request the exercise of this freedom in our favor and in the rational disfavor of others. When this happens not to be the case, we are still forbidden to act against the other's freedom, but rather, with the authority to share in it, we are given the duty to forgive and the privilege to reorient it to our – rightful – favor through dialogue, respect, and love.

The wife's body does not *belong* to her husband and the husband's body does not *belong* to his wife. Rather, each person owns his or her body but can be available to the other through love.

Discord does not only come because there is a problem. At times it comes because there has been no problem for a long time. Remain prudent.

Marriage is a reward when accepted unconditionally with love. It is a verdict when accepted conditionally for love.

Each time you neglect your partner, another is somewhere praising God for the opportunity given to do better.

Marry the person you wish, not the wishes of the person.

He who chooses a wife like a buyer who looks for the most fitting cloth with the best price would obviously suffer misfit. She who chooses a husband like a cloth seller who seeks the highest bidder would obviously fit mistakenly.

It is easier to bear a bleeding wound than a nagging wife. It is easier to cope with a migraine than with an angry husband.
Solitude is better to a deadly marriage.

The man marries, the woman makes the marriage. The man builds the house, the woman makes the home. The man brings the treasures, the woman brings happiness.

For men, marriage is a means. For women it is an end. Marriage is a journey.

A man marries when he has the means. A woman marries when the means are met.

Marriage is not about knowing great theories on love but about living the little experiences of love.

A good husband is better than a successful politician. A good wife is better than a successful and renowned feminist.

Marriage is not for emotional epileptics.

The fact is that soon after they married, each person thinks it could have been better with another person. Just after being with that other person, it is soon realized that there is another who is better. And after living with the best, you realize that everything is the same.

When a girlfriend becomes a wife, her privileges become rights. When a boyfriend becomes a husband, his rights become privileges.

Love is either what we feel or what we think. But what we think depends on what we feel and what we feel depends on what we think. Love is when our thinking approves our feelings and when our feelings approve what our thinking commands. Therefore, the object of love does not really justify our love, but rather the justification comes from what we approve of our thoughts and feelings.

A husband not a house band. A wife, not a knife.

After every honeymoon is a bitter sun. After every horny sun is a smooth moon.

Successful marriages and unsuccessful ones are often the same. They differ mainly in the way they are being perceived, because a successful one does not necessarily mean lesser problems and greater love and the unsuccessful one doesn't mean greater problems and lesser love. The main difference is in the way they are perceived, because perception shapes understanding. Understanding shapes behavior while behavior shapes decisions.

Marriage is not about conjectures on compatibility but about making little concessions about our incompatibilities.

Lesser divorces, so long as we admit that the two are NOT ONE and that the ONE IS TWO. This will reduce our *laissez-faire* and unnecessary mingling, thereby creating more chances for peace and happiness.

Hermeneutical error! When the two marry they don't become one! Each individual is a unique person, independent, free with a singular history and destiny. No rite or document can make such a fusion. Being one is only symbolic and pedagogical and not an essence!

Successful marriage	*Unsuccessful*
M = Mercy	M = Manager
A = Acceptance	A = Accuracy
R = Respect	R = Rules
R = Receptivity	R = Rigidity
I = Integrity	I = Intelligence
A= Assistance	A = Anger
G= Generosity	G = Greed
E= Engagement	E = Ego

MEDIA

When the media becomes business, information becomes a commodity, cosmetically blended to win the highest bidder, undergoing inflation or deflation depending on the profit margin. The truth becomes a luxury left only for a few hard working and non-tiring researchers.

Every media suffers from information deficiency syndrome (IDS) and every audience suffers from preferential deficiency factor (PDF). Because IDS and PDF are always at crossroads, media becomes a warlike jungle where values of truth, sincerity and honesty and sacrificed at the altar of interest.

Media against media. Every formal media faces challenges of marginalization from non- informal media tearing their audiences into a warfare of comprehension where only the toughest and prudent survive without casualties.

Information uses those who can't handle it properly.

Every media serves two contradictory roles: mediating and obscuring a message of the same information or reality. To know the truth, what is mediated is better understood from what is obscured.

The media is a friend to interest and an ally to information.

Media of death causes the death of media.

MERCY

Love is human. Mercy is divine.

Because love can make mistakes, I suggest that you get a love insurance from this accredited insurance company: Mercy Mutual.

MONEY

Any unmerited money corrupts and corrupts duly.

Where there is love of money there is also money for love.

The value of money is the money of value. In other words, money does not exists, value does.

Without money, relationships would be in constant discord. Without love these discords would perpetually be on fire.

We miss money simply by rushing after money. Rather, rush after excellence, talents, skills, and prudence. Then money would rush after you.

Love of money is the root of all evil. Lack of money is the tree of all evil.

In the world of money, money is the world.

Money is not the problem when we have it. It is unquestionably the problem when we don't have it.

There is enough money for everyone. All we need is the appropriate means of distribution through hard work, investment, and justice.

Use money or be used by money.

Love: color blind, money smart.

MORALS AND MORALITY: VIRTUE

Morality is not deontology. The first refers to the conduct of an individual with himself and society and the second refers to the conduct of individuals with regards to their profession. They are related in the *why* but differ in the *how*.

The law does not determine the morality of an action and the morality of an act is not determined by the law. It is determined by the right constitutive momentum of the will, the coherent, dynamic evolution of its means and the just orientation of its end.

It is not logical to say: "virtue is its own reward" else we would also say that evil is its own retribution. Virtue suffers diminishing returns when it is traded with its own reward.
Virtue is goodness beyond its own reward.

Morality is not behavioral comedy. Your moral maxim should not be a behavioral vault that aims to be a universal norm, but rather it should be a universal particularization aiming at perpetual betterment. Through continual confrontation with itself and others, it enriches and modifies itself. In other words, there is particularization of the universal not universalization of the particular.

Virtue is the only warfare that extinguishes the opponent without bloodshed.

Shame is the homage of vice to virtue. Guilt is the veneration of virtue by vice.

Morality or *moralitics*?

Morality: principles on how to behave.

Moralitics: study on morals, how men should behave. The first is standard, doctrinal, cosmetic, exegetic, and exclusive while the second is dynamic, theoretical, aesthetic, hermeneutical, and inclusive.

Virtue is the excellence of the mean, not the mean *par excellence*.

Operationally, morality is inspired by belief, shaped by economy, and appreciated by sentiments.

Anything that serves as a means cannot be absolute. If a means becomes absolute, it becomes its own end.

He who is not capable of anger is not capable of tolerance.
He who is not capable of patience is not capable of courage.

He who is not capable of pride is not capable of humility.

He who is not capable of solitude is not capable of friendship.

He who is not capable of selfishness is not capable of charity. Virtue is not the complete annihilation of vice but simply its neutralization at an acceptable level.

Love is the essence of virtue, but since virtue is often stratified and strategized in the vast dynamics of complex social interactions, it takes a great management skill to deal with each person, thus making the virtuous man more like a politician.
Virtue is also politics.

The intellectual verbosity on morality can be explained mainly in one way: too much talk on love implies the presence of hatred.
Too much discussion on peace is a symptom of tension.
Too much theory on justice implies the presence of injustice.

Morality is not the abundance of intellectual coherence and logic, but sufficiency and abundance of facts, because the presence of one often implies the shortage of the other.

We hold this as self-evident truth, that always:
Ignorance pays homage to wisdom through fear.
Evil pays homage to virtue through guilt.
Conspiracy pays homage to innocence through justice.
Yes, it is right to triumph by accepting not to triumph

when the opponent forges his triumph by his ability to keep hold of the law and the pulpit.

Love is not a virtue by itself. It is a concept that designates the constant practice of certain virtues: kindness, humility, forgiveness, hard work etc.

Every morality starts from the conscience [nature], grows through the mind [nurture], develops through society [law] and ends in the will [love].

Without the conscience there is no morality. Without the mind there is no conscience. Thus, morals are determined by the conscience-mind complex.

Every vow is characterized by love and fear, strength and weakness, tolerance and violence, fiction and friction, peace and war. That is why those who make them never avoid moments of great joy and great pain. Virtue is above the vow.

Strictly and paradoxically, many people are not virtuous because they believe that love suffices to be just. As such, they pay little heed to real, simple, and ordinary virtues under the pretext that love is their paramount virtue. But *who* is the determinant of the quality of such love if not themselves? And how do we determine the quality of love if not by the just application of virtues stated by conscience and law? Convinced that love is a virtue, they unduly undermine other minor virtues. Again, we should not take subtle words and our sentiments as references for virtue, for love is simply an idea that affirms the just practice of [all] other virtues and not a reality independent – in itself. Morality is not a romantic coherence of ideas and ideals, but a rough confrontation of facts with admissible practices.

At times, even nature is not natural. Adjusting it becomes natural and virtuous.

There is cowardice in every greed, there is courage in every charity, there is weakness is every pride, there is stupidity in every conspiracy, and there is fear is every act of selfishness.

Biology shapes psychology, psychology shapes behavior, while behavior shapes morality.

> Religion establishes morality through *an a priori* evidence.
>
> Policy establishes morality through an *a posteriori* evidence.
>
> Society establishes morality through an *a forteriori* evidence.

"Do not judge." But at times, refusing to judge is a bad judgment.

OPENNESS

Never be afraid to say openly and firmly what you don't like in others. Even when you continually praise them, it would not spare you from the verdict of misunderstanding, blame, insult, and violence.

PATIENCE

Never rush for food even if you are dying of hunger. Indeed, we are not alive because we eat most nor are we healthiest because we eat best.

Perseverance needs two virtues: patience and courage. The patience to wait for the expected outcome and the courage to fight for the expected outcome. Any perseverance that does not exhibit these two characteristics is either resignation or stubbornness.

Because our expectations are fruits of anxiety, they often fall short of reality. Expect modest results and be not anxious about things and the outcome would bring desired satisfaction.

PARADOX AND CONTROVERSIES

God created man on the seventh day. Nowadays, man is creating God on the seventh day.

Atheist and believer: The first rejects what he doesn't know while the second doesn't know what he projects. The first believes in himself in order to explore the unknown and the second believes in the unknown to explore self. In both, we find the unknown and self though they differ in the way they relate with these realities.

Salvation or redemption? Salvation is in creation while redemption is part of creation. God saved the world by creating it (salvation). He didn't create the world and later saw the need to redeem it (redemption).

The frustration of man lies in the paradox of the realization that he is blinded by his own ability to see, made insensible by his own feelings, made deaf by his own hearing, made tasteless by his multiple tastes. There is clarity only when reason is enkindled by true love.

God is an enigma for man. Man is an enigma for God.

It is not a crisis of politics but that of policy;
Not a crisis of religion but spirituality;

Not a crisis of sex but of love;

Not a crisis of knowledge but of wisdom;

Not a crisis of marriage but a crisis of those who marry;

Not a crisis of friendship but of friends;

Not a crisis of pleasures but of happiness and

peace;

Not a crisis of the true but of truth.

Politicians are stewards to economists;

Doctors are servants to pharmaceutical enterprises;

Workers are slaves to bankers.

The God of the people, not the people of God.

There is evil everywhere. It is greatest where it is least expected and apparently least where it is expected most. There is goodness everywhere just that it is most marketed where it is least practiced and least marketed where it exists most.

Most people practice religion not because they are determined to get better but because they are determined to feel better.

Those who give in sadness always receive in excitement.

People who are too zealous in one thing are often too timid in others.

He who has greatest capability to violence is venerated as peaceful, while he with the greatest vulnerability is marketed as violent. As such, being peaceful means being violent and being violent is simply due to vulnerable weakness.

The Noble Peace Prize and the International Criminal Court are like two hands of the same individual: it gives in one and takes in the other, rebukes in one and praises in the other, criminalizes in one and legalizes in the other, wages war in one and makes peace in the other.

When a diplomat smiles it is a sign of anger. When he laughs it is a sign of war.

PEACE

The attribution of peace to the possession of something or someone is a sign of vulnerability to insecurity and unhappiness, hence, our inability to truly possess them. Peace is the coherent, dynamic interaction between security and insecurity.

The greatest enemies of peace are those who refuse to fight for peace.

Truth is often on the side of the one who has the pulpit. Power is often on the side of the one who has the cash. Love is often on the side of the one who has the beauty. Peace is on the side of the one who is able to say no.

Whenever you are sad or angry, know that life is cheating on you, or you are cheating on life. Being at peace is a due and you shouldn't lose it for whatever reason.

Peace is better than happiness, happiness is better than joy, joy is better than pleasure, pleasure is better than leisure, leisure is better than boredom, boredom is better than inactivity, inactivity is better than death, death is better than the void.

Peace is in the faculty of the will.

Happiness is in the faculty of reason.

Pleasure is in the faculty of memory.
Memory fades. So does what memory cherishes. Reason judges, so changes what it weighs. The will determines, and so is the stability of what it is directed to.

Each time peace is considered a commodity bought and sold to the highest bidder, a terrorist is born.

Learn to rest: it is a gift of freedom and peace. But rest that is not from hard work is leisure and boredom – the challenge of laziness and idleness.

Conflict is natural. Peace is man-made.

PLEASURE

Indeed, there is so much suffering in this life. Pleasures were technically created to give us the wish to continue, while happiness was created to make us hang on even as things get tougher.

Nowadays, pleasure is a commodity available in sufficient amount for those who have the appropriate purchasing power. Because the demand is increasingly high, companies have volunteered to supply it in greater amount but have refused to lower the cost. Being produced by corporate organs, it means for each pleasure there is a tax value that is calculated by the assumed degree of satisfaction derived from it.

Pleasure comes from acquiring the things of desire.
Happiness is earned by avoiding the desire of things.

Pleasure is pain when we don't get the appropriate proportion.
Pain is pleasure when we have the appropriate proportion.
Suffering is the inability to make the difference.

Pleasure kills pleasure. Pain kills pain.

Pleasure is a feeling of the flesh experienced by the mind. Pain is a feeling of the flesh experienced by the mind. If it is in the mind that we experience pleasure, then wisdom is the greatest pleasure, and foolishness the greatest pain.

Suffering is the inability to make the difference.

POLITICS, INTERNATIONAL RELATIONS

U.P.O. not U.N.O. In the United People's Organization resources are united for the benefit of people while in the United Nations Organization, people are divided at the detriment of strategic resources.

International cooperation is better called international competition.

It is not the *end of history for the last man*. It is perhaps the last man at the beginning of his history. When history ends, it ceases to be history and becomes a spatial law.

It is not *the clash of civilizations*, but obviously the civilizations of clashes. Clashes at the intercivilizational sphere are only symptomatic of a civilization that has clashed with its own self.

Sovereignty is a dynamic attribute of the State that undulates depending on its corporate capabilities. In other words, sovereignty is a juridico-political myth theoretically defined to sustain corporate capabilities of the State. Therefore, sovereignty is fundamentally corporate.

International prescience exists not only in power dynamics between nations but equally between individuals from different nations who often think/behave, not so much with their individual compositions but with their nations prescience composition whose nationality they carry: psychology of international dynamics.

Deciphering international cooperation dynamics

COUNTRY	STRENGTH	WEAKNESSES	KEYWORD	ADVICE
FRANCE	Attractiveness	Quality	Duplicity	Distance
GERMANY	Severity	Rigidity	Complicity	Fortitude
CHINA	Affordability	Unsustainability	Secrecy	Stamina
AMERICA	Opportunity	Competitivity	Sustainability	Audacity
BRITAIN	Legality	Disproportionality	Precaution	Strictness
JAPAN	Efficiency	Transmissibility	Exclusivity	Smartness
ITALY	Flexibility	Complexity	Unpredictability	Prudence
RUSSIA	Security	Vulnerability	Power	Vigilance
CANADA	Neutrality	Partiality	Isolation	Clarity
EU	Efficacy	Ambiguity	Polycephality	Authority

Geopolitical soliloquy

Europe: 'I am suffocating between America and China, bitten by Russia. I need a breathing space...' Russia: 'I don't care what you say. With my arms and sufficient oil/gas, I remain dangerous despite the collapse of my beloved KGB.'

China: 'Buy and borrow more so as to be more dependent on me. Soon I would strangle all of you under my dragon strength.'

America: 'Power and glory are good but difficult to keep. However, I will do my best till you prove me the contrary.'

Africa: 'Unite me to live and prosper or remain divided and die for others to feast on me for their prosperity.'

Middle East: 'Allah, the all merciful is on my side, that is why I am blessed. I will be back again.'

Geopolitical curfew

This is the anatomy of a family whose future is suspended in a geopolitical curfew.

The first son is extremely strong and uses his strength to govern the family – America. The second son went on exile. On coming back he started fighting for birthrights. He is supported mainly by the weak – China. The third child united all her children to form a union in order to fight the elder two – Europe. The forth child refused his brothers and sisters, that is why they are not affectionate towards him. He agrees only when he is safe – Russia. The fifth child gave birth to fifty-four children who are divided and their parents refused to recognize them. That's why they sell all their resources in order to survive – Africa.

Other relatives do not struggle to be heir of the family but simply to be respected for who and what they are. The Father of the family is

Interest, the Mother is Politics while the House of the family is Strategy. To succeed and be safe in this family, one must thoroughly master the house

[strategy] and convince the mother [politics] to control the father [interest].

Every liberalism is based on the illiberal, while every communist socialism claims liberalism. Liberalism: people regulate government. Communist socialism: government regulates people.

The international scene is not anarchy or sheer order. It responds to the osmosis-effect whereby there is a flux obeying to the law of strategic influence.

Understanding the European Union

From numerical imperialism to digital imperialism

From territorial expansion to *ideo-spatial* expansion

From political colonization to economic colonization

From military occupation to corporate/strategic occupation

From collective scramble to collective gamble

From a normative point of view, America is a State – like all others. From a critical perspective, it is an empire. But in practice, it is a mega-machine that surpasses the classical functions of empires, making each citizen to become a tool that is carefully used to fuel its functioning.

Politics is always an object of discord because we always have ungrateful citizens and greedy politicians. Each party must be held tight by the law.

Every democracy falls prey into its own dictates
Every liberal economy is marked by its own protectionism

Making the public dislike politics or to be ignorant of it is another way to do politics.

Politics of insecurity

> Pakistan = Commercialization of insecurity
>
> Iran = Politicization of insecurity
>
> Syria = Fractorization of insecurity
>
> Somalia = Decentralization of insecurity
>
> Iraq = Instrumentalization of insecurity
>
> Israel = Paradigmatization of insecurity
>
> Afghanistan = Strategization of insecurity

Politics of security

> U.S.A. = Internationalization of security
>
> Europe = Internalization of security
>
> Russia = Commercialization of security
> China = Polarization of security

Politics needs intelligence, but it is not an intellectual problem

It needs strength, but it is not a question of force.

It needs dialogue, but it is not a question of lessons/sermons.

It needs actions, not necessarily reactions.

No government has ever fulfilled all its promises. If it ever does, politics would come to an end.

How can a conservative assure maximum interest without a progressive external and economic agenda? How can a progressive succeed without defending a conservative interest? Conservative or progressive makes no meaning on its own. What makes meaning is maximum interest.

Democracy and progress cannot be attained through a sociopolitical miscarriage. Everything must follow a due historicosocio-cultural process validated by tolerance and development.

Abuse of politics is a sacrilege and desecration to the sanctuary of common good.

Those who refuse to vote always hope for things to change but refuse to change their unchanging attitudes towards change.

Sovereignty is demonstrated by three main things: money, army and law. Sovereignty goes across borders when a currency, army and law go beyond national territory. In such a case, the nation ceases to be a simple State but becomes an empire. And if a nation uses a foreign currency, army and law, it loses all or part of its sovereignty and becomes a colony.

Definition of the State
Theoretical: territory, law and population. This is a material definition, which is imprecise.
Practical: money, law and army. This is an essentialist and functionalist definition, which is operational.

Types of State
Geopolitical States: Ossetia, Abkhazia
Empire States: U.S.A., Europe and soon China
Religious States: Is.ra.el, Vatican, Saudi Arabia

Kingdom States: United Kingdom, Morocco, Lesotho
Retailer States: Cameroon, Chad, Democratic Republic of Congo

Provincial or District State: Canada, Australia, and Jamaica

Colony State: Gabon, Senegal, Cote d'Ivoire

Power sharing is not between three branches but between four: the executive, legislative, judiciary and *financiary*. Anything less than this is a sociopolitical conspiracy against the people for the benefit of a few.

The sacred principle that defined the bases for international relations had been desecrated leaving the international scene to be a comedy show where only the greatest clowns prosper, flourish, are praised, venerated and rewarded.

Is the IMF a private bank of a few nations to structure and give loans to others at unbearable rates? While the World Bank a public development bank designed to share a portion of the dividends made from the IMF?

NATO against SATO.

International cooperation
The material comes from D.R. Congo

The labor from China,

The technology from the

U.S.A.

The innovation from Japan.

The market is the world.

Everyone needs everyone. All the thinker asks for is
equity in the distribution of profits.

When the triple entente initiated by NATO to convert
their enemies of the central axis into allies, their classical
allies were converted automatically into enemies.

Political science – as the art of blending the common
good – had long ago lost its essence when it failed to
demonstrate that modern States are simply
agglomerations of corporate organs linked together by a
tight string which is held by a few individuals who
control the money and the banks.

An ally is an enemy who protects our interest while an
enemy is an ally who doesn't protect our interest.

- *Difference between a State and an empire-State*

STATE	EMPIRE-STATE
Values: system of things they cherish	**Ideology**: monolithic perception – which is promoted beyond frontier
Economy determines money: determined by internal production	**Money determines economy**: going international determining economy
Security: strictly internal by its military and police services	**Security**: expansive, alliances with infinite intelligence services
Market: limited	**Market**: extensive, influence of currency
Cooperation: parallel-like and linear	**Cooperation**: web-like. umbrella

Comparison of virtues

Individual relations – persons	International relations – nations
Love	Selfishness
Meekness	Superiority
Temperance	Resistance
Peace	Tension
Longsuffering	Aggressiveness
Goodness	Eleemosynary
Faith	Suspicion
Joy	Anger
Gentleness	Rigidity
Truth	Lies
Conclusion	**Conclusion**
An individual who doesn't exhibit these virtues would meet problems, perish and go to hell.	A nation that does not exhibit these characteristics would be crushed, rendered poor and marketed as evil.

POVERTY AND THE POOR

The kindness that a poor man shows to the rich is service in order to be in good terms with the rich. The kindness that a rich man shows the poor is self-serving because he wants to be in good terms with himself.

Indeed, the poor are in trouble. Not only are they from the lower class, they are expected to be humble, to work hard for less, to be very thankful for the least they receive, never to provoke, to accept injustice, to praise the superior even in his errors. And when he dies of his poverty, he occupies a modest piece of land with the epitaph: 'Blessed are the poor.'

A poor government should blame its citizens. Poor citizens should blame their governments.

The highest justice that a poor can claim for himself is to get rich. Anything else is flattery.

People relate with the poor in terms of justice, and with the rich in terms of love.

There is nothing wrong in being poor. But everything goes wrong when we create our own poverty.

Those who consider their poverty as an exclusive responsibility of others often do not rise to fight for their prosperity. Accepting responsibilities and pledging never to repeat past errors is the royal path to progress.

A poor person is vulnerable to danger while poverty is danger in itself.

A poor person who is lazy and proud simply represents a situation where danger is in love with the dangerous.

Every poverty is lived as a broken dream. Every richness is lived as an imperfect dream.

The poor don't fear being in prison because poverty is a prison in itself.

What have I heard? If people are making their riches out of your poverty then it is noble to make your riches out of their abundance, legally.

Poverty is man-made. The poor are God-made.

A poor person who seeks pity for his condition would be rewarded with greater poverty. When he seeks justice fearlessly through hard work, sacrifice and fairness, he would be rewarded with greatness.

The best way to insult a poor man is to tell him: "Blessed are the poor."

A poor person is always the victim that the rich use to settle their differences. A poor nation is always the battleground that the rich nations use to settle their interests.

Fight against poverty not against the poor.

Material poverty is bad, structural poverty is dangerous, and anthropological poverty is lamentable.

Being poor is not an agreeable situation. Either others would always complain about you or you would complain about others.

POWER

Misuse of power is a sign of frustration. Love of power is frustration in itself.

All strength has its weakest point and every weakness has its point of strength. Success in battle does not often lie in conquering the strength of the other, but simply on strategy, based on keeping hostage the weakness of the other.

The strong man is he who refuses to fight when he knows he is weak. He agrees to fight when he knows that his opponent has been badly weakened.

Thrones are often full of thorns.

Ignorance of your weaknesses creates a misunderstanding of your strength.

Power is man-made. Authority is God-made. Power comes from below. Authority comes from above.

Generally, those who are physically very strong and courageous are often emotionally weak and cowardly. Those who appear to be physically weak and patient are often emotionally strong and resistant.

The discovery of the nuclear weapon only confirmed that *might is right*, writ and wit.

Gifts are more dangerous than weapons.

Never fight the wrong fight else your enemy would be a victor twice and you'll be defeated thrice.

It is better to be vulnerable by virtue of your strengths than be vulnerable by virtue of your weaknesses. The first will humble you, but the second will humiliate you.

PRAYER

Spiritual gluttony, religious verbosity, and avarice are as bad as not being spiritual.

Thank God that you are alive, and thank Him again that you will not be alive always. It is grace to have been here and peace to go forth elsewhere.

If singing is praying twice, then charity is praying thrice.

Sincere wishes come true when accompanied with daring actions. They remain a dangerous flattery when accompanied with lazy dreaming.

A life of truth and virtue is a living flame of prayer, thrusting itself through the burning furnace of society to the glorious firmament of the Most High.

A sincere prayer means honesty on its knees and at its best.

Prayer consoles us when we fall, strengthens us when we rise, sustains us as we move on, inspires us as we struggle, feeds us as we think, and comforts us as we suffer.

At times, our prayers anger God because we fail to do the right thing we are called to do because we think that we have substituted it with pious prayers.

PRIDE

A person should be deeply ashamed to boast of what does not duly belong to him, and should be even more ashamed if he refuses to be ashamed of his misappropriation.

Feeling basically superior is a vain attitude found in most empty people. Feeling basically inferior is an attitude found in those who do not recognize their greatness.

Anyone who strives to be at the center of attention always does so at the price of error.

PROBLEMS AND SOLUTIONS

Practically, *how* is more important than *why*. Theoretically and semantically, why is more important than how.

Unmerited progress often brings merited problems.

The easiest way to increase your problems is to look for solutions that don't last.

Refusal to be part of the solution imperatively makes us part of the problem. There is no neutral path.

No collective problem can be solved by independent individual solutions. No individual solution can be satisfactorily reached without a collective approach. If a problem affects everyone directly or indirectly, it makes everyone responsible in finding the solution.

Whosoever is at the origin of a problem is of least importance. Whosoever refuses to be part of the solution is of greatest danger to himself and to others.

You can hate those who do politics, not politics. You can hate those who practice religion, not religion. You can hate what people say about God, not God. Our hatred often leads to self destruction, because we often hate the wrong things for the wrong reason.

The more things are complex, the more they should be *complexified* in order to make them simple.

There are no ideal solutions to social problems, but there are ideal alternatives to every solution chosen.

Those who never get into trouble never know how to live in society. Those who always get into trouble never know how to let society live.

It is easy to hate those whom we don't know and love those whom we know. As such, we love and hate our knowledge or our ignorance of the other, not the person.

Those who see problems everywhere and in everyone always have a serious problem.

There is an alternative to every solution. Where there is no alternative, the only solution becomes a problem.

He who says a problem cannot be solved, commits an existential sacrilege, a reasoning profanation.
There is a solution to this problem. If we don't get the solution, it means we are the problem.

PRUDENCE

Believe no one who loves power. Trust no one who loves money.

Suspect anyone who loves sex. Fear anyone who loves all.

Cynicism is always characterized by frustration.

Neutrality is always characterized by partiality.

Indifference is always characterized by complicity.

Silence is always characterized by verbosity.

Equality is always characterized by imbalance.

Indecision is always characterized by resignation.

Greed is always characterized by despair.

Cowardice is prudence in the wrong place. Aggression is courage at the wrong time.

It is not right to be right all the time. At times, it is right not to be right.

Believe in your dreams but don't dream in your belief.

If you are told by someone that everything in you is good, then it is advisable to run away from that person. And if you see someone who seems to be everything good, once more, run away.

Evil in society is always greater than we see or detect. It is good to be more prudent than people can expect you to be.

The lesson we learn from our enemies is prudence. The lesson we learn from our friends is openness. But prudence makes us strong and openness makes us weak. There is no perfect enemy or friend.

You cannot make everything perfect without committing a perfect error.

When everything seems safe, that is when prudence is endangered.

When everything seems spiritual, that is when materialism triumphs.

When everything seems lovely, that is when the ego is ignited.

When everything seems good, that is when evil unmasks itself.

When everything seems beautiful, that is when the ugly unfolds. When everything seems coherent, that is when logic meets its frontiers.

When everything seems strong, that is when weaknesses awaken.

When everything seems to be said, that is when misunderstanding intrudes.

When something seems to be everything, that is when we start to be empty.

Do not believe in those who talk about their enemies in public places because they often dialogue peacefully in secret places.

Precaution prevents error. Too much precaution leads to error.

Obeying at the wrong time and wrong reason is equivalent to disobedience

Doing good at the wrong time and for the wrong reason is similar to evil.

Saying the truth at the wrong time for the wrong purpose is proportional to lies.

Unity at the wrong time and for an inappropriate objective is division.

Knowledge at the wrong place for the wrong reason is like ignorance.

Pleasure at the wrong place, time and reason is simply suffering.

Not everything is meant to work as planned. Not everything is destined to fail even without plan.

Accepting this and moving forward makes the difference called greatness.

Even when kindness is done with sincerity, it is always safe to consider the giver as a potential danger, especially when his own interest is involved. Danger is the ability to be naïve.

Timidity is virtue when it prevents us from doing wrong. Courage is evil when it cheers us to do wrong.

The greatest risk is when we think there is no risk. When we are aware of the risk, it no longer becomes a risk but a challenge to be faced.

It is better to be wrong by necessity than to be wrong by choice.

Let your prudence and patience never leave you. Your enemy, who watches you carefully, never takes leave of you.

Believe in the goodness of others. But do not ignore the evil they are capable of doing.

With diligence, offer the best you can for others.
With vigilance, deter the worst you can in them.

Keep your secrets even from your best friends because you don't know for how long they would be with you.

Correct your little errors, else others may use you to correct their great errors.

Do not be a paranoid of positive thinking.

It is good to hope on those whom we love, but imprudent to always believe in them.

Ride or be ridden.

Serve others before yourself. Save yourself before others.

There is always a reason to hate when we want to. There is always a reason to love when we want to. Generally, we often choose the one that serves our
   highest interest at the moment.

RELIGION/CHURCH

Monotheistic religions evolve through four important phases: 1) They start with mercy, discipline, love and charity. Gaining acceptance 2) they infiltrate society, politics and economy thereby defining the rule. As such, 3) becoming socially indispensable, they become intolerant, imperial, politicized and divisive, thus suffering mistrust from its people. As a consequence 4) they retreat strategically to be distant from state though remaining close, preaching tolerance between state, religion, and science. The first phase is called vigor (spring), the second phase is called splendor (summer), the third phase is called rigor (autumn) while the fourth phase is called anchor (winter). Socio-political dynamics of institutionalized beliefs.

Religion is the professionalization of spirituality like the State is the professionalization of society. Spirituality and society are fundamentals of man (God-made). Religion and State are functionalities of man (manmade).

The struggle to solve religious controversies always ends in more controversies. Thus, controversy is the structure of religion, reconciled by the string of belief.

In religion, the right way to make peace with an enemy is to reconcile with him. In politics the best way to make peace is warfare. But in any case, we often have an enemy, a warfare, a reconciliation and peace.

Exegesis often gives us the truth of what we want to hear while trans-exegesis often gives us the truth of what we don't want to hear.

Historically, the easiest way to wage war is to claim it in the name of God. If God is a warrior then every believer becomes immolate.

If the *raison-d'etre* of a belief in God is to make us God-like, then we who have chosen to believe should be ashamed of our choice.

A kind, merciful, and socially adapted atheist is better than a selfish, wicked, and socially misfit religious person.

A conviction is a hardline belief erected as truth to *cause a defense* or *defend a cause*. The first is to protect the individual from the insecurity of doubt and the second is to produce insecurity for those in doubt.

Any religion that goes out to defend its cause betrays its cause. Any religion that has no cause justly defends its cause. God is the defenseless defender of the defenseless cause.

Every religion suffers a complex of its own belief. Without a complex, it invalidates its own choice of belief.

Believers think the other blind and incomplete because the other thinks differently. The believer forgets the other thinks the same of him

When we believe in what we believe, we say that it is the will of God. When others believe in what they believe, we don't allow the will of God to be theirs but use reason and logic to declassify them. Is the will of God the validation of our choices, or is the will of God for others the result of our logical reasoning waged on others?

Why do they always fight and criticize each other? The thinker asked God, and He replied: "He who uses the fearless weapon of love and the defenseless shield of truth fights for me, anything else is against me."

He who believes in God and has never doubted a single instant would hardly be a good believer. He who refuses to believe and has never postulated His existence in an instant would hardly be a good atheist. The human condition is a perpetual apology of its own incertitude and weakness.

There is no innocence in religions. All have been stained by complicity, duplicity, and blood. Man should be saved before religion not religion before man.

Religion: worshiping God and shunning evil, not shunning God – of others – and worshiping evil – ourselves.

The Church is technically universal but semantically particular.
Buddhism is technically particular but semantically universal.

While some are proud of their religion, their religion is ashamed of them.

Atheist? That is a choice and makes no meaning on its own. Believer? That is a choice and makes no impact on its own. Respect for man, laws, social order, and peace are not a choice, but an obligation that makes impact and meaning. Therefore, let's talk about what puts us together and not what divides us.

Religion is not morality. Although morality is part of religion, it is above religion, because it goes beyond and across rites and beliefs.

Your belief makes little or no difference. Your action makes the whole difference.

Religion plays two roles that are opposites: 1) it connects man to God 2) by putting what is not God between man and God, thereby disconnecting God from man.

Historically, sacred texts have always been hidden or kept away from the general public. Today, despite a wide vulgarization of such texts, they still remain hidden or kept away from the public by the way they are interpreted. The first was hidden technically.
The second semantically.

Believers died for religion to start. Non-believers died for refusing religion. That is why it flourished.
Martyrs from within and from without.

Christianity is weakened by too much flexibility   of interpretation.   Islam is weakened by inflexibility of interpretation. Judaism is weakened by re-flexibility of interpretation. Interpretation!

God alone knows what is godly in religions.

The Christian, Muslim, Hindu and Non-believer all met at the tribunal of the Infinite in the afterlife. He asked them only one question: 'How did you treat fellow-man and yourself?' The forth was the first to qualify. Presently, God is still examining the case of the others.

Is God making a joke of religions or religions are making a joke of God? One thing is certain: one is making a joke of the other.

RESPONSIBILITY

It is better to be a loser in a game than a cheerful fan.

If a man lacks strength, let him have knowledge. If he lacks knowledge, let him have talents. If he lacks all, he becomes a danger to himself and not even his virtue would save him.

Those who are hard towards themselves are often soft towards others. Those who are soft towards themselves are often hard towards others.

Honesty is not truth. A person can be dishonestly truthful or honest in lies. Nobility is when honesty meets truth.

It is sad to be a gambler and sorrowful to be used for gambling.

It is not enough to seek the best in every situation, but to be the best in what we seek in each situation.

It is indeed sad to be serious all the time. It is sorrowful never to be serious.

Keep the promise even when the promise does not keep you. Nobility is honesty at its best.

The best way to be influential is to do everything without being influenced.

The envy to remain young is motivated by our inability or unpreparedness to accept what time brings. Being what we ought to be frees us from envy of youth or fear of age.

To the most successful: pleasure
To the most perseverant: happiness
To the most truthful: peace

Those who are quick in making promises are smart in breaking them.

What we call our rights is often a duty to others, and what we call our duty is a right to others. Failure to respect our duties is an abuse of the rights of others, and abuse of our rights is the misuse of the duty of others.

Every greatness comes at a great price.

It is not only important to know what you want. It is more important to know what you can get and how to get it.

RESPECT AND DIGNITY

It is a misfortune and a shame to receive respect and reputation that you don't deserve.

It is a shame to lose the sense of shame.

It is dangerous to give more respect than a person deserves.

It is easier to humiliate a person with gifts more than insults.

The greatest insult a person can give to himself is to misuse his talents. The greatest respect that a person can do for himself is to invest in his talents for the benefit of others.

We receive people the way we conceive them. The way we receive them shows how much we receive or deceive ourselves.

It is disrespectful to desire so much respect.

Even if an elderly man has lost his dignity, show him due respect so he doesn't suffer twice.

If a friend disappoints you, he deserves less trust, but more respect. Remain noble.

If a man should surrender his dignity in exchange for a favor, he would certainly be stripped of his dignity and humanity. But if he should surrender his dignity in order to save man, his dignity would be restored and his humanity enriched.

Respect for God is respect for man, while respect for man is respect for God.

Never praise a person beyond his merits. It would insulate his merits. Never criticize a person beyond his limits. It would expose your weaknesses.

RHYME

Zeal is real deal for pearl.

Waiters hardly wake while those who wake hardly wait.

The fist does not make the first,
The pest cannot make the best,
To heed does not make the head,
The wrong does not make the strong,
The rite does not make the right.

Haughtiness is naughtiness.

RICHES

Riches bring us pride when duly merited. They bring shame when unmerited.

The poor hunger for what they don't have, and the rich hunger *from* what they have.

It is not possible for everyone to be rich. It is not possible for everyone to be poor. But it is possible for everyone to be satisfactorily well-off.

Poverty means we are indebted to ourselves, Riches mean we are indebted to others.

The rich easily normalize what is penal, while the poor easily suffer penalization as normal.

SCIENCE AND PHILOSOPHY

From a physical point of view, cause produces effect. From a metaphysical point of view effect produces the cause.

Behind every explicitly defined scientific theory there is an implicitly undefined philosophy. Scientific coherence is simply a manifestation of philosophical indispensability. Science is practical philosophy, while philosophy is theoretical science, though evolving as science and philosophy respectively. Science seeks evidence to understand truth while philosophy seeks truth to understand available evidence. In other words, truth is the discovered evidence while evidence is an uncovered truth.

Science creates the means, and arts create the end. But what is the means without the end and what is the end without the means?

The reasonable is above the rational.

The more refined a theory, the more obscure it becomes. The less refined it is, the clearer it seems to be. Epistemology fluctuates between the clear and the obscure.

The ultimate objective of all sciences is often unscientific: leisure, pleasure, happiness, peace, comfort. Why blame those who are less or not scientific? Their objectives are equally the same. They differ only in the method.

Development depends on the progress of science while science depends on the progress of arts. Theoretically, art is above science. Practically science is above arts, but development is a scientific art or an artistic science.

Technology makes life easy by making man difficult.

SECURITY

Every national defense has an impact on international offense. Every national progress has an impact on international imbalance. The international sphere is a jungle of no-man's land governed by diplomacy.

Every security has its insecurity challenges. Real security is not the ability to produce tough security, but the inability to produce inoffensive opponents.

The strength of a country's military is proportional to its industry. If it has no corresponding industry then it is just an equipped foreign market whose wars would not only be for its destruction but for the triumph of the supply country, which rejoices in the prosperity of its market.

Every military doctrine is based on the idea of deterrence. Paradoxically, there is no complete deterrence without an impact on offense. Security undulates between deterrence and offense brought to equilibrium by diplomacy.

If national security is ensured at the cost of sovereign security, then national security has become a threat to the nation itself.

These are the things that provide us security.

For the State: Army, banks, and law.

For the Family: Love, money, and dialogue.

For the Individual: wisdom, hard work, and discipline.

Security means that which can prevent or provoke insecurity. As such, every security can turn into insecurity.

For every organization to survive, it needs a protective vault that serves as the base for its security.

In the family: 'we are of the same blood' – affection

In society: 'We are under the same law' – justice

In politics: 'Our ideas are good for others' – influence

In business: 'Spend less, gain more' – interest

In religion: 'It is the will of God' – belief

Anything that comes as a threat to a nation always succeeds with the help of the citizens. If only our citizens really love this nation sincerely, we would need less or no army for its security.

SERIOUSNESS

People don't take each other seriously because they know that they have alternatives in a world of billions. But this is contradictory because those who don't take themselves seriously always know that they don't have an alternative life. We treat others the way we treat ourselves.

No matter how serious a fanatic is, a comedian is still better than him. In other words, a fanatic is just a mistaken comedian.

'Now, let's be serious.' This is another symptom of lack of seriousness.

The danger of being too serious is that we get tired thrice: tired from the weighing emptiness of this existence and tired by taking such emptiness as a serious matter, and of course tired again by being unable to make the difference.

Work smart not hard. But to work smart, you most start by working hard.

Be natural in everything you do. Artificiality often creates casualties irreparable by time, money and hard work.

SEX, PASSIONS, AND EMOTIONS

Emotion is a dissolved reason in delight. Reason is a contracted emotion in detection.

Our emotions are hidden in reason while our reason is hidden in emotions.

Is homosexuality a moral, social, economic, biogenetic, religious, criminal, health, or political *problem*? It is simply an *issue* of conformity. But who defines conformity? He who first normalizes his nonconformity.

For women, sex is a means. For men, it is an end.

Is sex the desire for pleasure or the pleasure of desire? Now, if sex is a desirable desire, then it is simply a desire. In other words, it is a desire of desire for desire.

Anyone who always gives privileges to his emotions would definitely work against his own emotions.

Sex life is directly related to a people's morality, sociality, economy, and politics.
Morality: what is approved or not, how family ties are made. Sociality: how we interact, or speak, what we believe, our style of dressing, our dance.

Economy: determines our motivation to work, what we buy, how we save and commercialize. Politics: has impact on population, modifies our interest in public and private life and shapes their engagement in life as a whole. Not knowing the impact of our sex life makes us to be a danger to society.

A woman makes love when she desires. Anything else she calls it violence. A man makes love when he has the means. Anything else he calls it a surprised privilege. However, the desire always attracts the means while the means always creates the desire.

When we study love, sex, and marriage scientifically [neurogenetic approaches, for example], the truth is that nothing gets better fundamentally. They help only to give us sufficient justifications why we should quit or complain without sorry or worry... or to remain when we derive fun in it. Scientific gambling continues.

Some people consider their bodies to be too precious and beautiful to let it engage in sex. But when they conquer with reason they are conquered with emotions.

Sex is necessary when it is absent. When it is present we don't see its value. Sex is always missing between its presence and absence.

179

To men, sex is a human right. To women saying 'no' is part of women's rights.

To men, it is about performing. To women it is about performance.

Changing one's sex does not make a person better in any way. It only changes the perception that one is getting better.

SILENCE

The most important figure in mathematics is zero. The most important form of language is silence.

So far, we have learnt more and even better from silence than from these endless speeches and sermons.

Silence is louder than noise.

Silence is not the absence of sound. It is the sound of absence.

Never talk much about people and don't let them talk too much about you, if you want to live in peace.

Silence is not only the refusal to speak unnecessarily. It is also the refusal to act unnecessarily.

Music is harmonized sound while silence is harmonized music.

We talk a lot because we often do not find the right words to use, and do not say what we want to say in the right way.

Silence is not the inability to speak. It is rather the ability to excellence of speech.

Noise has never been a virtue even if you have good reasons for creating it.

SOCIETY

Everyone seems to be absorbed in society but in reality isolated from it.

Society is sustained on two arguments: *argument of principle* and *argument of facts*. The first disposes while the second proposes. Both indirectly impose. If the first wins, there is order but great injustice. If the second wins, there is justice but disorder. Balance exists when the principle *factualizes* and when the facts *principalize*.

There is no rationalization of society without a strictly rational public administration, and there is no public administration which is sufficiently rational without a rational and dynamic politics, and no rational and dynamic politics is possible without a rational and stable law. There is no rational and stable law without a rational and fixed vision for the maximum peace and security of all.

The quest to be what you *ought* to be is often infringed by what you *want* to be, altered by what you are *capable* of being, and influenced by what society *permits* you to be.

Societal trigonometry has three angles of 60 degrees called business, politics and religion. The sum of these angles is 180 degrees called interest.

So far, man has invented two types of tools: an instrument and a weapon. The first for his progress and the second to oppress. The difference between societies is based on the type of tools they have.

In every family, there is always someone who seems to be a misfit, but together as a family, they are protected and given solace. In every society, there is something that seems to be a misfit, but together as a society, we fail to protect *it*.

Politics is the crucible on which the matrices of society are built.
Hating politics is hating society. Hating society is hating man.
Hating man means hating oneself.

The most irresponsible person in society is he who does not seek to know how he is governed and what happens to his stocks [taxes]. Being blind, he becomes a threat to everyone.

In this fearless battle of society, good intentions are also neglected while hard work can equally be sanctioned. Those who survive are the ones who apply smartness fearlessly in the battle ground of fate and destiny.

In intercultural dynamics, the melting point does not necessarily follow the direction of what has the best values, but rather that which weighs disproportionately in favor of the culture with the highest purchasing power and with greater strategic influence.

Social violence is directly proportional to social inequalities.

When love enables us to get what we want, it is called strategy. When it enables others to get what they want it is called a technique.
Strategy and technique make those who love agents of social craft.

How are the two related and I will describe the nature of the relationship.

> Between master and servant = dependence
>
> Between priest and faithful = surrender
>
> Between lover and beloved = flattery
>
> Between friends   = compromise
> > Between enemies   = suspicion
> >
> > Between married couples   =sacrifice
> >
> > Between business partners = interest
> >
> > Between politician and citizen= gambling
> >
> > Between man and woman   = comedy
> >
> > Between humans   = strangeness

Between religions = blasphemy

Between God and man   =mercy

Martyrdom means to be good beyond the point that a society can contain. Society has its own logic in the acquisition and propagation of values.

A society survives by integrating what enriches it and resisting what impoverishes it. Integration without resisting leads to extinction. Resisting without integrating leads to boredom. Without integration and resistance, the culture becomes a mental relic possession only archeological virtues.

Those who are allergic to criticisms are of extreme threat to everyone.

The most sacred thing in human interactions is the common good – not love.

The law of society states that for every grouping, the cohabitation force is derived by weighing the strength of each individual or subgroup which is consensually juxtaposed as pros and cons, multiplied by the binding agent – legality – plus the dividend of the leading structure. All divided into its various components of interest to form a product of the common good.

The most dangerous people in society are those who think that they are too good for society.

Strategically, it is not man that makes society but society that makes man.

With elections, we shall get rid of public charlatans. With wisdom, we shall get rid of false prophets. With thinking, we shall get rid of emotional constipation and indecency

With governance, we shall get rid of public pirates.

Upon examination, it appears that the main problem with the drug crisis is the culture crisis. Culture is combated by culture. That is why arms, prisons, laws, and deaths would not be able to solve this problem.

Culture: perception, reception and deception. All culture is a perception oscillating between reception and deception.

Permanent organized structures survive not by merit of what is virtuous in them, but by what is violent. Society – strategic violence. State – legitimate violence. Religion – symbolic violence. In the historic dynamics of religions and sociopolitical evolutions, violence is virtue.

The culture of killing kills culture.

SUCCESS

Victory is good. Defeat is bad. Knowing how to cope with each is great.

Organically, we owe our success to others and our failure to ourselves.

After working hard through true application of goodwill towards success, it can still happen that you fail and at times even fatally due to three reasons: a) Your success can be judged as a threat,
unconsciously or not, to the security of others. b) Society is not so much about goodwill but about good opportunities and rough undertakings. c) Finally, we must admit that some people, even when we suspect the least, could be simply wicked with the lust to see evil triumph. In all, success is a due that is worked for and which often comes through many privileges that we didn't work for.

Without passion, no significant accomplishment of reason can establish distinction. Without reason, no amount of passion can establish accomplishment but rather extinction.

Success is not just an accomplishment. It is a task, a duty – as we progress in it, and a debt – when we have accomplished it.

You must succeed! If you are tired of moving forward, reduce the distance. It is still success in its own proportion.

Progress means working for others. Technically, it means working for ourselves.

Opportunity is not a block of success that we luckily meet on our path. It is rather the path of daring where we skillfully unblock the obstacles we meet.

Son, to succeed, let wisdom be your father, hard work your mother, discipline your brother, honesty your sister, prudence your neighbor, and truth your lover. Good luck.

None of our accomplishments is definitely perfect. Where we end others begin to go even further. But refusal to accomplish something less perfect from which others can continue is a perfect error.

Where everyone gets tired, do your best to go an extra mile. Success and excellence are just about that.

We need the success of others more than their failure.

Generally, success is when opportunity meets our strength. Failure is when misfortune meets our weakness.

The success of others often benefits us directly or indirectly. The failure of others often harms us directly or indirectly. If only we knew how much our welfare depends on the welfare of others, we would desire their success more than ours.

When a person succeeds, every argument is fabricated to justify his success. I call this the *success-argumenteffect*. When he fails, every argument is coined to justify his failure. I call this the *failure-argumenteffect*. But beyond the success-argument-effect and the failure-argument-effect there is the logical argument based on sustainable effect, for no success is beyond failure and no failure is beyond success. Success is simply the ability to suspend failure while failure is simply the state of suspended success.

You don't need to be the best among all others in order to succeed. Rather, you need to be the best of yourself and you will succeed and surely have the best.

Every success is a merit and a credit.

Success by association is equivalent to failure by dissociation.

Every failure is an opportunity for correction while every success is an opportunity for perfection.

Never be too prudent because you want to succeed.

Never avoid all risk because you want to be safe.

Success is when risk meets opportunity.

Do not complain that others block you from progressing because others equally look at you as a blockage to their progress.

There is no progress that is infinitely expansive. Sustainable progress knows how to limit its progress in a viable pattern.

If you work hard without thinking hard, you are working in vain. If you think hard without working hard, you are thinking in vain.

Nothing changes for you until something changes in you.

SUFFERING

The greatest suffering a person can undergo is to refuse to suffer for the just cause at the right time. Surely, one of the greatest pleasures a person can experience is to refuse pleasure for the just cause at the right time.

He who takes pleasure in the pain of another person would certainly feel pain in the pleasure of the other; because he emotionally depends on the other, he becomes a danger to himself.

Humans cannot stop suffering because they cannot stop their desires. Happiness is the ability to cope with suffering.

It is sad not to know what suffering is.

It is not important what sufferings you have gone through. It is what you do with what happens to you that matters

No matter the sufferings, stand on the right side. It is the nature of things not to be the same.

When a suffering person laughs, it is not because he is happy but because sorrow at its deepest ebbs laughs at its own sorrow.

Is it the ungodliness of God or the inhuman-ness of humans that is the cause of this issue? More likely both.

THINKING

The human mind is not material or immaterial but simply *inmaterial*. A problem cannot be solved empirically without being solved conceptually.

The mind is the foundation of all subtle games. It must be flattered that it knows, so that it should continue to search and think; that it loves so that it should persist in being passionate and kind; that it is needy and desiring so that it should find pleasure in gratification; that it is automated so that it can find delight in consciousness; that it is spiritual so that it should aspire to the divine lights of light. Without this game, nothing makes sense.

Nothing exists as complete, exclusive rationality or irrationality in spatio-temporal dynamics. In fact, there is often a degree of irrationality in rationality and some degree of rationality in irrationality. Correct judgment should be based on the establishment of the appropriate balance between the two.

Think sharp, act wise, live smart, talk low, and die silently.

The thinker was asked: "What do you see: a half-filled cup or a half empty cup?" And he replied: "I see only a cup." "Do you see a man as half good or half bad?" Again, "I see just a man." We think wrongly because we ask wrong questions.

Thinking is either one dimensional: dogmatic

Two-dimensional: paradigmatic

Three-dimensional: theoretical

Four-dimensional: synchronic

Think kindly of one another like the thinker is thinking about you.

TIME

Time is not a reality in itself. It is simply a dimension with which we appreciate reality.

Time is our best ally because it is with it that we can do whatever we want. It is equally our worst enemy because it comes only once.

Strictly speaking, time does not exist in itself. It is a concept that refers to the rate of change. In other words, only change exists in itself not time but we say time when we want to appreciate the nature of change. Without change, there is no time although change can still occur.

The only wasted time is the one spent without love.

What is the time of *time*? Present presence or perpetual presence.

Two types of time: motional or emotional. The first is the rate of change while the second is the change of rates.

TOLERANCE

Religious intolerance is not so much about discrediting other belief systems but also about crediting one's own belief system exclusively and with absolute authenticity.

Religions are intolerant towards one another simply because they are intolerant towards God.

Generally, we are tolerant when the exercise of the freedom of others benefits us and intolerant when we get no benefit from it. Tolerance is the ability to accept loss so long as it permits the just exercise of liberty.

Those who are intolerant always believe that their own faults are mild, justifiable, and tolerable.

Too much tolerance is a violation of tolerance.

Tolerance is not the permission that we give to others to exercise their rightful freedom. It is the acceptance that the exercise of the freedom of others is not a privilege of our permission.

Anyone who thinks that tolerance is a favor offered to the other
– to exercise a rightful freedom – commits a strategic violence.

Violence is either the abuse of strength or the overuse of weakness. Tolerance means the synchronized use of strength and weakness. That is, strength is tolerance with regard to the other while weakness is violence with regard to oneself due to its offensive defenselessness.

TRUTH

Organically, truth is a noun while true is an adjective, but materially truth is an adjective while true is a noun.

The distance between truth and true is *truity*, measured by *epistemometrics*.

Truth is not the complete, systematic compressibility of the whole but simply the systematic circumscription of the all encompassing within the limits of the perceptible and the comprehensible.

Truth is heretical in any context where falsehood is normalized.

Truth:
When truth becomes a conceptual framework putting together a group who admit its coherence, it is called a theory.
When it is a binding force compelling many to follow, it becomes a law
When it is a conviction built on belief to harmonize meaning, it is called revelation.
When it is a conviction, theoretically erected into a law, it becomes a dogma.

Once more, truth is human perceptibility of spatiotemporal coherence in historic dynamics.

If the principle of uncertainty is certain, then it means that uncertainty is epistemological while certainty is epistemic. Truth is the coherent dynamics between the epistemological and the epistemic.

He who says there is no truth makes false his own argument and he who says all is vanity makes vain his own affirmation.

He who defines truth defines justice, he who defines justice defines morals, he who defines morals defines the values of things, he who defines the value of things defines the economy, he who defines the economy defines power, and by defining power he uses it to get all he wants. The greatest warfare that exists is the one based on truth. For those who define it always use it to get all other things. Truth is also strategy and strategic.

Either we admit that truth is constant while our perception of it is mutable, or we admit that it is mutable while our perception of it is constant. Again, truth is the coherent, mutable constant.

Truth is not cosmetic but aesthetic, not arithmetic but geometric, not chronological but synchronic, not doctrinal but hermeneutical, technically rough but semantically smooth, not the summit of sense but the sum of sense, not perfect but ideal.

How do we consider truth?

> To the Hebrew it is eternal.
> To the Greek it is dynamic.
>
> To the Russian it is power.
>
> To the French it is discursive.
>
> To the Chinese it is progress.
>
> To the German it is ideal.
>
> To the African it is historic.
>
> To the American it is pragmatic.
>
> To the English it is rationalistic.

Truth is not coherence. What therefore is coherence? It is the establishment of acceptable and accepted links of facts with itself and/or with perception.

Truth is one, not oneness.

Truth is human. True is divine.

Truth does not always triumph but thrust does. Right does not always triumph but might.

Does truth make sense on its own if it is not placed on the crucible of love, tempered with kindness and tolerance?

Truth is the perpetual mutable in a mutable constant on human perceptibility in a perceptible coherence.

Demonstration

Key Concepts: perpetual mutable, mutable constant, human perceptibility and   perceptible coherence

So,   i. Perpetual mutable * mutable constant

= mutable (perpetual. Constant)

ii. Human perceptibility * perceptible coherence

=   perceptibility   (human. Coherence)

Thus above (i),(ii) =

$$\frac{mutable \ (perpetual \, . \, constant \quad)}{perceptibility \ (human. \, coherence \quad)}$$

⇓

$$\frac{mutable}{perceptible} \cdot \frac{perpetual.constant}{human.coherence}$$

But, perpetual constant = human coherence

Therefore, $\quad \frac{mutable}{perceptible}(human\ coherence)$

Given that, $\frac{mutable}{perceptible}(human\ coherence)$ = Coherent
Constant

So, Truth = Coherent constant

Thus, T = Cc

Nothing is as simple as truth, and no truth is as coherent and simple as this formula.

TRUST

It is not wrong to trust no one. But trusting no one means inability to trust oneself.

Trust does not kill suspicion.

Trust the one unexpected to be trusted. Trust not the one who expects to be trusted.

Trustworthy people are difficult to find because we are not trustworthy.

Trust is an asset. Distrust is a liability.

Trust is a guarantee with no collateral security.

Who can we trust?
>   In England: Newton
>   In U.S.A.: Abraham Lincoln
>   In China: Mao
>   In S. Africa: Mandela
>   In India: Gandhi
>   In R.D. Congo: Lumumba
>   In Italy: Garibaldi
>   In France: Descartes

In Germany: Luther

In Greece: Aristotle

In Cameroon: Um Nyobe

In Is.ra.el: Jesus

Any other person is a suspect who cannot be proven innocent after trial.

UNDERSTANDING

There is always a linguistic deficiency when we describe others with words and there is always a practical surplus when we discover them in reality.

We do not automatically love those who have done something good to us because love is a choice. We do not automatically hate those who have done something wrong to us. Hate is a choice.

Those who think that nothing can be appropriately done without them would realize, regrettably, that things could go better without them.

With belief, anything false can be made true.
Without belief, anything true appear to be false. One of the main differences between men depends on what and how they believe.

Happiness is sustained by suffering.
Success is sustained by failure.
Strength is sustained by weakness.
Pleasure is sustained by pain.
Knowledge is sustained by ignorance.
Wisdom is sustained by foolishness.
Only love is sustained by love.

Everybody is capable of understanding anyone.

Misunderstanding is only a result of diverse interests.

What divides us is not understanding, but interest.

Where business stops, politics starts. In other words, politics is advanced business. Where politics stops religion starts. In other words, religion is advanced politics.

Among us nature has its favorites. Being favored by nature means we are indebted to others. Not being favored by nature means nature is indebted to us.

If we are really good, why are we not loved by everyone? If we are really bad, why are we not hated by all others? If we are the enemy of the enemy and the friend of the friend of the enemy, it means that we are not different from the enemy and should rather make of him an ally.

It is not good to agree all the time. It is not wise to disagree all the time.

Give money. It will be used to get power.

Give power. It will be used to get money.

Give beauty. It will be used to get love.

Give love. It will be used to get beauty.
We want things not because we need them but because they enable us to get other things.

The greatest charlatans come in the name of truth; Thieves come as financial consultants; Worst enemies pretend to be friends.

There is no naïve question, only naive answers; no naïve love, only naive lovers; no naive religion, only naive believers.

Do not be surprised that people don't share your opinion. Rather, be astonished why you don't share theirs.

Choice is a possibility that restricts other possibilities.

If everyone believes in a lie, it becomes truth. If no one believes in the truth, it becomes a lie.

Irrationality is the frontier of reason and the reasonable becomes the summit of reason.

Only God is above you. You would understand this truth only when you fearlessly rise above and conquer yourself.

God is not a gambler but men have never ceased to gamble in the name of God, declaring victory when the dice turns to their favor.

The heart always finds someone to love and another to hate. The one we hate is used as a victim of strengthening the link to the one we love. The one we love is used as a means to explain why the other is hated. Why gamble where there is no game?

There are some people whose greatest fault is by virtue of their natural characteristics, unless they prove the contrary. There are others whose merit is the veneration of some natural characteristics unless they are proven the contrary. When nature becomes the center, man becomes the periphery, revolving around the gravitational force of his own delusion.

The unjustified kindness towards those who don't really merit it is often due to our unjustified selfishness towards those who don't deserve it.

If we remove the word "love" from our vocabulary, nothing would change. On the contrary, we would be enriched with the knowledge of knowing exactly what motivates human interactions and how to control them.

When it comes to business, even the enemy is made a friend so that our interest can be secured. When it comes to politics, the friend is made an enemy so that our interest can be secured. When it comes to religion the friend is made an enemy until he shares our belief, and the enemy is made a friend just because he shares our belief.

When you make the best of the misfortunes bestowed on you by others, they would be surprised at the unknown opportunity they offered you. But when you keep mourning about your misfortunes, they'll rejoice for their job well accomplished.

Too much doctrine indoctrinates.

All have problems. Succeeding is the ability to see an opportunity in the difficulties of others.

One thing is certain about man: his incertitude. Faith and reason are operational choices made to govern uncertainties.

Zeal, not zealots.

Behind every secret there is a secret. Behind every curtain is another curtain. Inside every trick is another trick. And inside the game is another game. Naivety is seeing only the first secret, curtain, trick, or game.

Strictly speaking, people are not interested in the truth. They are more interested in the belief that comforts them. That is why a truth against such belief is often rejected, while a lie in conformity with a belief that comforts is welcome.

Biography: what do we choose to write and what do we choose to leave out? The real person is found in the lines that were left unwritten.

Seek to understand and you'll be understood. Seek to be understood and you'll misunderstood.

We cannot expect the best from others while being the worst of ourselves.

UNITY

What unites us is our diversity and what divides us is our unity.

Division keeps unity together.

Unless man becomes one, God would refuse to be one.

People feel more secure when unity is established through separation and insecure when unity is established through general togetherness. In other words, our unity is often a strategy against the unity of others.

Being together and togetherness: the former always results in casualties of anger, exclusion, seclusion, greed, envy and pride. The latter is when casualties are suspended by humility, love, truth and tolerance.

Our division profits all others greatly except ourselves. Our unity harms them very dangerously.

VANITY

What do we gain when we gain everything according to our desires? What do we lose when we lose everything?

Nothing.

What do we know when we admit that we know everything?

Nothing.

What do we gain when we are loved and venerated by everyone?

Nothing.

We cannot properly appreciate the value of things if we cannot understand or relate to the idea of *nothingness*.

Social networks: cybernetic verbosity

A person who tells you that he knows that the truth about the will of God is a poor magician that has ran out of tricks and is about to exhaust his last skill in blinding you to your extinction.

Vain struggle:

We struggle to save our title more than we struggle to save our names.

We struggle to save our personalities more than our persons.

We struggle to save our jobs more than our lives.
We struggle to save our beliefs more than the truth.

We struggle to save justice more than the just.

We struggle to counter more than to encounter.

We struggle to save money more than letting money save us.

Finally, we struggle to save God more than letting God save us.

A vow that cannot be kept should not be made.

VICTORY

The victory of the other is not yours. It can be beneficial only when you use it in creating your own victory.

WAR

War is simply a business with inflated prices. Now, if we have unjustifiably inflated prices, we would not be wrong to think that it is a war waged against us indirectly.

War breeds war. Peace breeds peace.

What we tactfully deter with arms we often unskillfully embrace through culture, business, diplomacy, and knowledge.

Anything that can be gained through war can be gained through cooperation and peace. Anything that can be gained through violence can be gained through love and non-violence. Humans are simply impatient.

Every war has a trick, and the ultimate trick lies in the hands of he who sponsors the war – financially, technically, strategically, symbolically,   and ideologically. We know them.

Where there is trade there is non-war because trade is already war.

The lesson that men have learnt from wars is their ability to fight more wars.

A war becomes just only when we accept that it is unjust, thereby refusing to fight it.

Warfare

Politics is warfare where the enemy is blackmailed, tarnished, and marketed as unfit, substandard and outdated; legally obliged to bow before his persecutor who eats the lion's share. As he goes away shamefully, he continues to murmur: 'I will be back again.' Business is warfare where the enemy is subjected to infinite needs and desires, technically compelled to continually buy from his aggressor while thanking him to have satisfied his vain needs and taken all his money. Society is warfare where the enemy is thrown to the lower class and tactfully convinced to remain there so that he would perpetually work for his oppressor while thanking him to be the source of his hope and salvation. The world is warfare where the enemy is subjected to poverty and dependence through an international maneuver and strategically compelled to sell all his resources at a miserable price to his conqueror as a sign of reconciliation and pardon, and begs for aid that would sustain him at a long run in underdevelopment.

Religion is warfare where the enemy is bound to accept that he does not know the 'true' infinite, that he is deeply evil or pagan and that true salvation for him is only

217

'here'; he is skillfully led to bow before his predator through rites where he surrenders wealth, will, and creativity in exchange for peace and happiness.

Love is warfare where the enemy is subjected to complex passions versus psycho-emotional hysteria, romantically compelled to seek refuge in the arms of his extinguisher through a consensus and as they walk together he is obliged to always say: 'I love you' even though he knows he would still be hurt again.

Life is warfare where the enemy is subjected to poverty, misery, illnesses, blames, accusations and misfortunes, openly obliged to seek security in the territory of his extinguisher who administers drugs – to the glory of pharmaceutical enterprises that get the profit, seek justice from the law – to the glory of the lawyer who gets hired, seeks religious security – to the glory of the parish priest who gets the tithes, secure a job opportunity – to the glory of the manager who enjoys the labor, where he saves a little – to the glory of the banker who manipulates the cash, that would sustain him in a slippery way towards his corpse – to the glory of the carpenter who produces the coffin. May his soul rest in peace.

Warfare is when the aggressor falsely accuses, violently, and mercilessly terminates his opponent– for no just cause, he emerges as the peace maker, the lover of justice, the holy chosen one, the innocent one, thereby gaining unrivaled veneration, power, recognizance as a pillar of all, both from within and from without. War is raw.

The Geneva Convention on War regulated how war should be fought. But war is basically inhuman, and bad. A convention on war is - the highest form of legalization of crime – of the inhuman. When war becomes business, the criminal becomes legal and the legal, criminal.

WISDOM

If you say no to wine, drugs, cigarettes, promiscuity, power and noise, wisdom will make you her friend.

When you boast of your wisdom you automatically cease to be wise.

It is not wise to expect things to always be the way we expect them to be.

Wisdom is prudence in practice. It is eloquence in words. It is truth in the mind.

You can get everything with strength except wisdom and love.
Wisdom is strength while love is above strength.

Wisdom is a Fountain – from above, that overflows with coherence at the pace of prudence into the receptacle of silence to the stream of love.

'Be wise and stand for the just cause, for when the time comes, even if you are dead, your corpse would be exhumed, cursed and disgraced publicly for its mediocrity and foolishness.'

Never seek to be too wise. You will get bored by it.

The difference between foolishness and wisdom is like the difference between God and man: one is made in the image of the other, but they differ in beauty.

Litany of wisdom

Mathematics is a systematic articulation of figures that enables us to rationalize the real, while wisdom is the realization of a rationale through rigor that enables us articulate our systems.

Biology is the study of life, which enables us to know why we die, while wisdom is the study of death enabling us to know why we live.

Physics is the study of the laws of nature, which enables us to know how to overcome them, while wisdom is the study of how to overcome the laws of nature, enabling us to know how to create and live with them.

Theology is the study of God, which enable us to believe while, wisdom is the study of beliefs which enable us to be Godlike.

Economics is the rationalization of production in society, which enable us to live well, while wisdom is the distribution of production in a society, which enable us to live rationally.

Chemistry is the study of the nature of particles, which enable us to know how to interact them while wisdom is the interaction of particles that enable us to know their nature.

Psychology is the study of human behavior in order to know how to enrich it, while wisdom is the study of enriching humans to enable them behave better.

Geography is the study of the natural graphics that enable us to understand our place in nature, while wisdom is the appreciation of our place in nature which enable us to gravitate naturally.

Politics is the control of power which enables us to enact policies for society, while wisdom is the enactment of better policies that enable us to better control power.

WOMEN AND MEN

Women hate lies but love liars. Men love lies but hate liars.

Men make things complicated, women are complex, and being in love is complexity.

Woman is the center of gravity around which the world revolves.
Any surrender to gravity means no motion, no progress. Complete separation from gravity means no weight, emptiness. Peace and progress are sure only when we keep a sustainable distance from the center called respect.

Woman is a mystery to man. Man is mysterious to woman.

Men and women reason alike. That is why, in any case, they often find a point of compromise. The first thinks vertically from *above* to *below* while the second thinks vertically from *below* to *above*.

When a woman misbehaves to her advantage, she says it is her right. When she misbehaves to her disadvantage, she says her rights have been violated.
When a man misbehaves to his advantage, he calls it smartness, manliness, bravery, or courage. But when he

misbehaves to his disadvantage he says life is unfair, or that society is wicked.

Women believe in what they hear, that is why they often suffer from what they see. Men believe in what they see, that is why they suffer from what they hear.

Men and women often agree on the objectives but disagree on the means.

Women often object to the sentimental role attributed to them, but practically, when they are deprived of such roles, they still object it vehemently to them. When the exercise of such roles yields maximum interests, they long desperately to do more.

Feminism is theoretically coherent, but feminists are practically incoherent.

Every 'single-mother' seeks to see other ladies as 'singlemothers.'

When a man relies on the help of a woman, he would be at the mercy of unpredictable emotions. When a woman relies on the help of a man, she would be at the mercy of predicted emotions.

Men claim that good women are difficult to find, but they forget that the bad ones are numerous because of men. Women complain that serious men are difficult to find, but always forget that the unserious ones have been spoiled by them.

Men easily get angry, and women easily get jealous. But jealousy leads to anger while anger leads to jealousy. Both are two sides of the same coin.

A woman's 'no' is never definite, and her 'yes' is never definite. What is definite is her unpredictability. A man's strength is never certain and his weakness is never certain. What is certain is his ability to surprise himself and those around him.

Put two women together, something would conspire. Put two men together, something would perspire. Put man and woman together, something would transpire.

Women readily believe those who flatter them because they often flatter others. Men easily agree with those who are not sincere to them because they are hardly sincere to themselves.

The attraction of women to men is shown by respect. The attraction of men to women is shown by admiration.

Women always search for serious men. But give them one, and they would refuse, turn away to someone else. Men always search for beautiful and understanding women. Give them one and they would ride past in search of another.

Do not ask what secret a woman has. She is a secret by nature.
Do not ask a man what problem he has. He is a problem by himself.

Women admire men for what they are. Men admire women for who they are.

Beware of any man who says he does not love women; he is a danger to all women. Beware of the woman who says she does not love men; she is a threat to all men.

Men judge the beauty of women from what they feel, while women judge the handsomeness of men from what they think. When it comes to choices, men are more sentimental while women are more rational.
When it comes to assuming those choices, men are more rational while women are more sentimental.

When a woman receives something from a man, she sees it as a confirmation that she can get more. When a man receives something from a woman, he sees it as a puzzle to be solved because he could have had less.

Each woman has at least five advisers and the most trusted of them are her gossipers. That is why her decisions are always unpredictable. Each man has at most two advisers: his friend and his interest. The most trusted is his interest, which is why his decisions are often predictable.

A true man must have a cause for which he dedicates his intelligence, an activity for which he dedicates his strength, and a lover for whom he dedicates his love. Anything less makes him an accomplished paralytic and anything more makes him to be a refined psychotic.

A true woman must have a domain where she consecrates her wisdom, an area where she dedicates her talents, and a lover for whom she surrenders her love. Anything less makes her a successful sclerotic and anything more makes her a joyful neurotic.

How does a woman measure her strength? By her ability to seduce.

How does a man measure his strength? By his ability to subdue.

However, to subdue is to seduce and to seduce is to subdue.

A man cheats when he has the means. A woman cheats when the means are met.

A faithful man is he who has not yet been caught, while a faithful woman is she who has not been proven otherwise.

Men weigh their confidence using the *front scale*, while women weigh theirs using the *back scale*.

When a woman is angry, that is when she says the truth. When she is in love, she lies. When a man is angry, he lies. When he is in love, he says the truth.

Every woman, no matter how ideal, always has her weakest spot where she seems unbearable. Every man, no matter his goodness, always has his weakest spot where he seems bad. And at times, those with ideal qualities often have the greatest weaknesses. The verdict of being human is the idealness of not being ideal.

A man who relies on the help of a woman makes a concession of his manhood by which he would be held captive until his sentence is pronounced where he is then handed over to his executioners for humiliation. A woman who relies on the help of a man makes a confirmation of her womanhood by which she would be held hostage until she makes a concession - where she is then liberated through approbation.

We know that angels don't have any sex, but all the angels we know are masculine. This is suspicious and discrimination against women.

All women are the same, but they need to be treated differently.
All men are different but need to be treated the same.

When a woman prays, she asks God for three things: a good husband, money and good children. When a man prays he asks God for three things: wealth, intelligence to acquire more wealth, and wisdom to manage his wealth.

Men rule the world from above. Women rule from below.

Men have interiorized the masculine representation of God which they've devised to boast their self-proclaimed superiority. As such, they position themselves favorably in all honorable positions in politics, business, and religion while leaving the hard, less honorable and inconsequential role to women under the pretext that it is the will of God.

Men hardly shed tears. Not because they don't grieve but because they accept their grief as part of their existence.

229

Women easily shed tears not because they are often in grief, but because they don't see it as part of life.

The only man who understand a woman is he who admits that he has never understood, does not understand and will likely not understand but continues to love unconditionally.

Being a man is a science; being a woman is an art.
Being human is metaphysic.

WORLD AND MODERNITY

The world is technically rough but semantically smooth, structurally diverse but systematically uniform, diplomatically horizontal but strategically vertical, economically parallel but socially cyclical, religiously to the right but spiritually to the left, physically complex but metaphysically simple, historically temporal but spatiotemporally eternal.

Who controls the money of the world governs the world.

Learning the secrets of how our world is governed leads to sadness. Understanding how it is really governed leads to sorrow. Modern man has surrendered by choosing drinks, sex and drugs, but sorrow is better than shame.

Man has transformed the world to be a beautiful place for himself, but has remained ugly for the world.

It is not difficult to change the world for the benefit of man. It is rather difficult to change man for the benefit of the world.

Has man ever been friendly to fellow man?

When he claims his freedom, the other becomes a subject.

When he canonizes himself as just, the other is demonized as a suspect.

When he assumes he is cultured, the other is marketed as a barbarian.

When he decides to believe, the other is stigmatized as a pagan. When he proclaims himself civilized, the other is diagnosed as primitive.

When he defines truth, the other is advertised as an impostor, heretic.

When he chooses vocabulary, the other is decreed ignorant. When he defines value, the other is asked to accept existential bankruptcy.

When he defines law, the other is dammed the lawless law breaker.

When he defines beauty, the other's is mocked as a caricature of aesthetic jargon.

When he defines culture, the other's is slammed as a useless fabric of no value.

When he defines the exclusive *we,* the other is marked as the exclusive *they.*

Has man ever been friendly to fellow man?

Two major factors determine a real civilization: the first is the maximum promotion of culture, intelligence, and health (positive factor). The second is through the minimization of unjustified violence from within and from without (negative factor). The first criterion is validated in all civilizations, while the second is relatively absent in all civilizations. We are still in search of a real human civilization.

America is a challenge to itself and the world.
China is challenging itself and the world.
Africa is being challenged by itself and the world.
Europe is resisting challenge from itself and the world.
Only change is constant.

Even when things happen haphazardly, always consider them as designs that emanate from someone to modify the status quo and create an objective, by creating winners and losers.

The world changes constantly, but man remains the same.

Everyone seems to be ignorant of everyone simply because everyone is watching everyone.

In the screen era, nothing would remain the same: the satisfaction we get from it creates our dissatisfaction. The joy we derive from it creates our pain. The comfort we extract from it confirms our boredom. Fiction would continue to be in conflict with our daily frictions, envy would be the mode and the final verdict would be the perpetual misconception that happiness is *there* not *here*.

In the real world, humans are unreal.

Man is not a necessity for the world, but the world is a necessity for man.

How has the world been perceived?

      Ancient time = Philo-centric

      Middle Age = Theo-centric

      Enlightenment = Techno-centric

      Modern = Money-centric

All are characterized by vertical visions but differ only on the perspective. The world has not changed, only the way in which it is being perceived.

This is our world:

      The splendor of the American life,

      The honor of the English life,

      The rigor of the German life,

      The glamour of the Spanish life,

      The clamor of the French life,

      The rumor of the African life,
      The labor of the Chinese life,

The vigor of the Japanese life.

World geopolitical comedy:

> The actors are in the West,
>
> The players are in the East,
>
> The distracters in the Middle East,
>
> The pitch in the South,
> The spectators in the South West
>
> The referees are in the Middle-East of the West.

WORRY

The things that bring people together are the same things that pull them apart. Be not too anxious about these things.

There is worry in everything because everything worries. But to be worried about everything is weary and dreary.

The young find it easy to disobey because, being young, they think they have a second chance. The old find it easy to sanction because they think they have nothing to lose. Generational affirmation makes sense only through intergenerational confrontation, dialogue, and search for harmony.

Worry not. Worry naught. Knot the worry.

When we put together fate, destiny, luck, opportunity, grace, weaknesses, strength, will and misfortune, we have a sum of an individual suspended on the slippery tangent between misery and greatness. This is called anxiety. Fear of misery is anxiety. Desire for greatness creates anxiety. Indifference is anxiety in itself.

Why do we always complain about those who complain? We often use vice to spot vice.

It is unfortunate when we struggle at all cost to tell man that he is fortunate to be man. His whole existence is emptiness, strife and worse still, worries about such emptiness.

Those who sit and worry would be rewarded with greater worries and troubles. Those who rise and fight justly would be rewarded with peace, happiness and prosperity.

Misery: Ignorance, laziness and dishonesty.

YOUTH

Be patient with old people, they never choose to be old, just as the young never choose to be young. Each age is a difficult challenge on its own for those who enter into it and a mystery for those who have not entered into it.

Youth is a risky opportunity.
Adulthood is an *opportune task*.
Old-age is a slippery gift.

Youthfulness is the same everywhere. The main problem with our young people is that they think they are different.

The best thing a young man can do is to invest for his old age, and one of the best things an old man can do is to enjoy the investment of his youth.

Young people are characterized by anxiety, which leads to stress.
Old people are characterized by stress which leads to anxiety.

The anxieties, worries, restlessness, and dissipation of youth make us to believe that youth is a verdict of vengeance bestowed on men until they conquer it with the maturity of age.

It is our obligation not only to be serious with ourselves, but to sincerely assist this young generation into a responsible *humanhood* through sacrifice, discipline, education, hard work, and justice. This is the greatest sign of solidarity to them, their future, which we pray, should be better than ours.

Youth like comedy because youthfulness is comedy.